Jack Nicklaus Says It All!

First there was *The Swing from A–Z* . . .
then *The Short Game and Scoring* . . .
Now, SHORT CUTS TO LOWER SCORES

Are you inadvertently cheating yourself at your own game? Now golf pro Jack Nicklaus offers his personal winning strategies to help you solve the most common—and most difficult—problems encountered in the game!

- Finding a driver that matches your swing
- Keeping your grips in good condition
- Making friends with long irons
- The perils of over-experimenting
- Under-clubbing—a worldwide problem
- Avoiding "hero" shots
- How to stop "skying," "thinning," and hitting "fat"
- Playing straight in wet conditions
- The Nicklaus formula for hitting farther

AND MUCH MORE!

PLAY BETTER GOLF III

Most Pocket Books are available at special quantity discounts for bulk
purchases for sales promotions, premiums or fund raising. Special
books or book excerpts can also be created to fit specific needs.

For details write the office of the Vice President of Special Markets,
Pocket Books, 1230 Avenue of the Americas, New York, New York
10020.

PLAY BETTER GOLF

VOLUME III

SHORT CUTS TO LOWER SCORES

Jack Nicklaus

With Ken Bowden
illustrated by Jim McQueen

POCKET BOOKS

New York   London   Toronto   Sydney   Tokyo   Singapore

An *Original* Publication of POCKET BOOKS

 POCKET BOOKS, a division of Simon & Schuster Inc.
1230 Avenue of the Americas, New York, NY 10020

ISBN: 0-671-72765-6

First Pocket Books printing May 1983

15   14   13   12   11   10   9

POCKET and colophon are registered trademarks of
Simon & Schuster Inc.

Printed in the U.S.A.

Contents

Introduction

One of the most frustrating—and fascinating—things about golf is its impermanence. One day you "have it" and the next you don't. This is true of every element of the game from driving the ball to holing it out. I've gradually improved in just about every area of technique over the years, but never in all the 30 and more years I've played golf have I been able to hold top form for more than comparatively short periods. Everything always goes in cycles—peaks and valleys. That's one reason I gear my playing schedule around the major championships. Knowing it's impossible to maintain top form for an entire season, I try to build and tune my game for the events that are the most important to me.

The number one reason why no golfer can stay at his or her peak indefinitely is that human beings aren't machines. Our ability to exactly repeat a certain set of actions is limited, and thus our abilities as shot-makers are bound to fluctuate. This is compounded by the tendency, present in all of us, to eventually overdo or exaggerate whatever we have found to be successful. In terms of the golf swing this tendency often creeps up on us subconsciously, but it is none the less destructive for that. And, when it has done its dirty work, reality has to be faced: if we want once more to play up to our maximum potential, the rebuilding or retuning process must begin all over again.

This book, the third in my PLAY BETTER GOLF series, is designed to help take a lot of the pain out of this most basic of golfing challenges by providing answers to the shot-making problems all of us encounter at some time or another. As before, I've tried to be as clear and precise as possible, and also in this case to organize the material for quick and easy problem-solving reference. However, as almost every element of shot-making is covered, I feel this book could also be very helpful as an overall guide for anyone seeking all-around improvement at the game.

As with the previous volumes in the series, all the articles herein were created originally for worldwide distribution to newspapers by King Features Syndicate of New York, and once again I offer my thanks to the people at King for their fine efforts in that respect.

Jack Nicklaus

PLAY BETTER GOLF

Part ONE

Preparing to Play

1

Getting Properly
Equipped

Correct Clubs Make Golf Easier

YOU CAN'T "BUY" A GOLF GAME, BUT YOU CAN MAKE THE GAME EASIER BY ENSURING THAT YOUR CLUBS FIT YOUR PHYSICAL CAPABILITIES AND SWING STYLE.

JM

FOR EXAMPLE, IF DIRECTION IS YOUR CHIEF PROBLEM, THEN STIFFER SHAFTS MIGHT TAKE SOME OF THE BEND OUT OF YOUR LONG SHOTS. CONVERSELY, LIGHTER OR MORE FLEXIBLE SHAFTS CAN HELP THE WEAKER GOLFER ADD VALUABLE YARDAGE — AND ALSO FLY THE BALL HIGHER.

ASK YOUR PRO FOR ADVICE AND FOR HELP IN EXPERIMENTING.

Fit Driver to Swing Style

HAVING TEE-SHOT TROUBLES ??

LOOKING FOR A NEW DRIVER ??

DON'T BE HASTY... TALK TO YOUR PRO AND EXPERIMENT UNTIL YOU FIND ONE THAT MATCHES YOUR SWING CHARACTERISTICS -- ESPECIALLY YOUR <u>TEMPO</u>.

IF YOU SWING HARD AND FAST, YOU'LL ALMOST CERTAINLY DO BEST WITH A FAIRLY STIFF-SHAFTED CLUB. IF YOU ARE A RELATIVELY SLOW AND EASY SWINGER, A FAIRLY "SOFT" SHAFT IS LIKELY TO SERVE YOU BETTER. REMEMBER, THE OBJECT IS TO FIND A DRIVER WEIGHT AND SHAFT FLEX THAT ENABLE YOU TO DELIVER THE CLUBHEAD <u>SQUARELY</u> WITHOUT MAKING SWING COMPENSATIONS.

Experiment with Grip Thickness

IF YOU'RE SERIOUS ABOUT GOLF, FIND A WAY TO EXPERIMENT WITH VARYING GRIP THICKNESSES.

YOU MIGHT BE SURPRISED AT THE DIFFERENCE A SLIGHTLY THINNER OR FATTER GRIP CAN MAKE TO YOUR GAME.

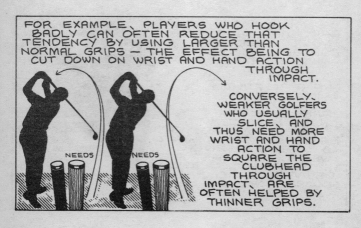

FOR EXAMPLE, PLAYERS WHO HOOK BADLY CAN OFTEN REDUCE THAT TENDENCY BY USING LARGER THAN NORMAL GRIPS — THE EFFECT BEING TO CUT DOWN ON WRIST AND HAND ACTION THROUGH IMPACT.

CONVERSELY, WEAKER GOLFERS WHO USUALLY SLICE, AND THUS NEED MORE WRIST AND HAND ACTION TO SQUARE THE CLUBHEAD THROUGH IMPACT, ARE OFTEN HELPED BY THINNER GRIPS.

NEEDS   NEEDS

Keep Your Grips in Good Condition

THE CONDITION OF YOUR CLUB GRIPS CAN BEAR HEAVILY ON HOW YOU SCORE.

CLUB SLIPPAGE IS FATAL AT ANY POINT IN THE SWING, AND IT'S BOUND TO HAPPEN SOMETIME IF YOUR GRIPS ARE SLICK OR DRIED OUT.

ALSO, WORN AND SLIPPERY GRIPS WILL FORCE YOU TO HOLD THE CLUB TOO TIGHTLY, INHIBITING PROPER SWING ACTION.

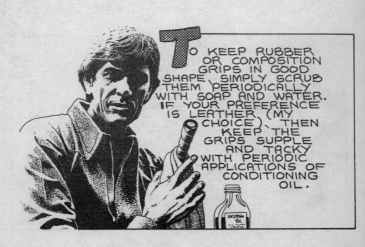

To KEEP RUBBER OR COMPOSITION GRIPS IN GOOD SHAPE, SIMPLY SCRUB THEM PERIODICALLY WITH SOAP AND WATER. IF YOUR PREFERENCE IS LEATHER, (MY CHOICE), THEN KEEP THE GRIPS SUPPLE AND TACKY WITH PERIODIC APPLICATIONS OF CONDITIONING OIL.

Check Flange to Solve Sand Problems

HAVING BUNKER PROBLEMS?

CHECK YOUR SAND-WEDGE.

IF YOU'RE DIGGING TOO DEEPLY, IT COULD BE THAT THE CLUB HAS INSUFFICIENT FLANGE TO LET IT "BOUNCE" THROUGH THE SAND EASILY.

CONVERSELY, IF YOU'RE "BLADING" OR CATCHING THE BALL THIN, IT'S POSSIBLE THAT A CLUB WITH A SHALLOWER FLANGE WOULD TAKE SOME OF THE PAIN OUT OF THOSE SAND SHOTS.

SHOW YOUR CLUB AND YOUR BUNKER ACTION TO THE PRO, AND TAKE HIS ADVICE.

2

Getting More
from Practice

When in Trouble, Go Back to Basics

GOING THROUGH A SLUMP?? TRIED EVERYTHING AND NOTHING WORKS??

WHEN THIS HAPPENS — AS IT DOES TO ALL GOLFERS AT TIMES — THE FASTEST REMEDY IS USUALLY A LESSON FROM A TEACHER WHO KNOWS YOUR GAME.

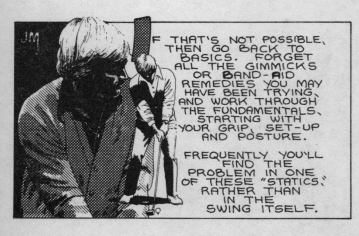

F THAT'S NOT POSSIBLE, THEN GO BACK TO BASICS. FORGET ALL THE GIMMICKS OR BAND-AID REMEDIES YOU MAY HAVE BEEN TRYING, AND WORK THROUGH THE FUNDAMENTALS, STARTING WITH YOUR GRIP, SET-UP AND POSTURE.

FREQUENTLY YOU'LL FIND THE PROBLEM IN ONE OF THESE "STATICS," RATHER THAN IN THE SWING ITSELF.

Play, Don't Practice, After Layoff

STARTING GOLF AGAIN AFTER A LONG LAYOFF?

DON'T GO OUT THE FIRST TIME AND BEAT A THOUSAND RANGE BALLS: YOUR MUSCLES AREN'T READY FOR IT AND THEY WILL DEFINITELY PUNISH YOU!

INSTEAD, DO WHAT YOU'VE BEEN DYING TO DO, WHICH IS **PLAY**, NOT PRACTICE. USE AN OUTING OR TWO ON THE COURSE TO REKINDLE YOUR ENTHUSIASM, AND ALSO TO TELL YOU WHAT AREAS OF YOUR SWING OR GAME PARTICULARLY NEED WORK. BY USING THIS EXPERIENCE TO CREATE A PRACTICE PLAN, YOU CAN THEN GO SERIOUSLY TO WORK WITH SOME **CLEAR** OBJECTIVES IN MIND.

Practice Regularly, Thoughtfully

Knowing **HOW** TO PRACTICE IS AS IMPORTANT AS ACTUALLY DOING SO. FOR INSTANCE, FREQUENCY IS MORE IMPORTANT THAN QUANTITY, AND **THOUGHT** IS EQUALLY IMPORTANT AS PHYSICAL EFFORT IF YOU WANT TO GET MORE FROM PRACTICE THAN EXERCISE.

MOST AMATEURS HAVE A TENDENCY TO HIT TOO MANY SHOTS TOO FAST TOO HARD WHENEVER THEY GO TO THE DRIVING RANGE.

IF THAT'S YOU, PLACE YOUR PRACTICE BALLS THREE OR FOUR PACES AWAY FROM YOUR HITTING SPOT, SO THAT YOU ARE **FORCED** TO PAUSE AND THINK BETWEEN SWINGS.

Give Swing Changes Time to Work

IF YOU'VE RECENTLY HAD A LESSON, OR ARE WORKING ON SOMETHING YOU BELIEVE TO BE SOUND THAT YOU'VE FIGURED OUT FOR YOURSELF, THEN BE PATIENT — **GIVE IT TIME.**

REMEMBER THAT, EVEN FOR THE TOUR PROS, ANY SWING CHANGE, HOWEVER SLIGHT, TAKES WEEKS OF WORK BEFORE IT FEELS COMFORTABLE AND BECOMES "REPEATABLE."

MANY AMATEURS NEVER REACH ANYTHING LIKE THEIR FULL GOLFING POTENTIAL BECAUSE THEY ARE FOREVER TRYING SOMETHING DIFFERENT IN A SEARCH FOR INSTANT IMPROVEMENT. BELIEVE ME, THERE IS NO SUCH THING, JUST AS THERE ARE NO "SECRETS."

IF YOU WANT TO PLAY BETTER AT THIS GAME, THE ONLY ANSWERS ARE THE **FUNDAMENTALS + PERSEVERANCE + HARD WORK.**

Don't Over-Experiment

BIG DANGER WHEN A PRIDEFUL GOLFER DEVELOPS A PERSISTENT FLAW IN HIS GAME IS OVER-EXPERIMENTATION IN SEARCHING FOR A CURE.

SUCH A COURSE WILL OFTEN DESTROY YOUR GOOD MOVES FASTER THAN IT WILL RESOLVE YOUR INITIAL FAULT.

WHENEVER I'VE GOTTEN TO A POINT WHERE I COULDN'T RESOLVE A PROBLEM WITHIN MY BASIC SWING FUNDAMENTALS, I'VE ASKED JACK GROUT FOR HELP. BEFORE YOU'VE EXPERIMENTED YOURSELF INTO TOTAL CONFUSION, A VISIT TO A TEACHER WHO KNOWS YOUR GAME COULD SAVE YOU A LOT OF PAIN, TOO.

Make Friends with Long Irons

IF YOU'RE SCARED OF LONG IRONS, HERE'S A WAY TO GET FRIENDLY WITH THEM.

HIT A FEW EASY 9-IRONS TO FIND YOUR IDEAL TEMPO AND RHYTHM. THEN HIT A BATCH OF 4-IRONS USING EXACTLY THE SAME SWING.

DO THE SAME WITH THE 8-IRON/3-IRON. AND THE 7-IRON/2-IRON.

TWO OR THREE SESSIONS LIKE THAT AND YOU'LL LOSE YOUR FEAR — AND IMPROVE YOUR SCORE.

Work on Your Short Game, Too

PLAYING IN PRO-AMS, I SOMETIMES GET THE IMPRESSION THAT THE BETTER AN AMATEUR'S LONG GAME, THE WORSE HE'LL BE AT RECOVERY SHOTS.

IF THERE'S ANY TRUTH IN THIS, IT'S PROBABLY DUE TO AN IMBALANCE IN PRACTICE TIME.

GOOD FULL SWINGERS PROBABLY SPEND SO MUCH OF THEIR PRACTICE EFFORT WORKING ON THE BIG SHOTS THAT THEY LEAVE INSUFFICIENT TIME OR ENERGY FOR THE SHORT GAME.

THAT'S A COSTLY ERROR IF YOUR ULTIMATE CONCERN IS SCORE RATHER THAN SWING ESTHETICS.

3

Improving
Your Attitude

Test Your Golfing Honesty

CONVINCED YOU ARE HITTING THE BALL AND PUTTING BETTER THAN YOU'RE SCORING?

WELL, THERE HAS TO BE A REASON, AND A LITTLE SELF-ANALYSIS MIGHT IDENTIFY IT.

TEST YOUR GOLFING HONESTY.

ASK YOURSELF HOW MANY SHOTS YOU WOULD HAVE SAVED IF YOU NEVER LOST YOUR TEMPER, NEVER GOT DOWN ON YOURSELF, ALWAYS DEVELOPED A STRATEGY BEFORE YOU HIT, ALWAYS PLAYED WITHIN YOUR OWN CAPABILITIES.

THE ANSWERS — IF YOU CAN BE TRULY HONEST WITH YOURSELF — MIGHT SOLVE MOST OF THOSE SCORING PROBLEMS.

MISUNDERSTANDING GOLF'S TERMINOLOGY CAN SLOW DOWN PROGRESS FOR THE BEGINNING PLAYER. SWING "PLANE" AND "ARC" FREQUENTLY SEEM TO BE CONFUSED — EVEN, SOMETIMES, BY EXPERIENCED GOLFERS.

YOUR SWING PLANE IS THE ANGLE AT WHICH YOUR ARMS AND THE CLUB SWING RELATIVE TO VERTICAL OR HORIZONTAL, AND THE CLOSER IT IS TO MIDWAY BETWEEN THE BETTER YOU'RE LIKELY TO PLAY.

YOUR SWING ARC IS THE PATH DESCRIBED BY THE CLUBHEAD WITHIN THAT PLANE — AND THE WIDER IT IS THE BETTER.

Precision Counts More Than Power

MANY MEN WOULD BE MUCH BETTER GOLFERS IF THEY COULD PLAY WITH A LITTLE LESS MACHO — IF THEY COULD EMOTIONALLY ACCEPT THE FACT THAT GOLF IS A GAME OF PRECISION RATHER THAN POWER.

415 YDS
PAR 4

LONG HITTING IN ITSELF HAS NEVER WON A TOURNAMENT THAT I KNOW ABOUT, BUT THE EFFORT TO HIT LONGER THAN NECESSARY TO SCORE WELL SURE HAS LOST AN AWFUL LOT DURING MY TIME IN THE GAME!

THAT'S WHY YOU'LL SO OFTEN SEE ME TEEING OFF WITH LESS THAN A DRIVER, ESPECIALLY ON TIGHT HOLES.

Focus on Remedies, Not Faults

AVOIDING FEAR OR ANGER AFTER A BAD MISHIT OR MISJUDGEMENT IS MAYBE GOLF'S SINGLE GREATEST CHALLENGE.

ONE TECHNIQUE I'VE FOUND SUCCESSFUL IS TO FORCE THE ERROR OUT OF MIND BY MAKING MYSELF IMMEDIATELY FOCUS VERY HARD ON THE NEXT SHOT IT REQUIRES ME TO PLAY.

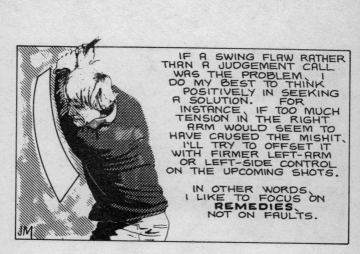

IF A SWING FLAW RATHER THAN A JUDGEMENT CALL WAS THE PROBLEM, I DO MY BEST TO THINK POSITIVELY IN SEEKING A SOLUTION. FOR INSTANCE, IF TOO MUCH TENSION IN THE RIGHT ARM WOULD SEEM TO HAVE CAUSED THE MISHIT, I'LL TRY TO OFFSET IT WITH FIRMER LEFT-ARM OR LEFT-SIDE CONTROL ON THE UPCOMING SHOTS.

IN OTHER WORDS, I LIKE TO FOCUS ON **REMEDIES**, NOT ON FAULTS.

Take More Club More Often

WANT THE NEXT GOLF SEASON TO BE MORE FUN THAN THE LAST?

MAKE AND STICK TO A RESOLUTION TO TAKE **ONE MORE CLUB THAN YOU FIRST THOUGHT OF** ON EVERY TEE SHOT TO A PAR-THREE, AND EVERY APPROACH TO A PAR-FOUR, AND I PROMISE IT WILL BE.

6-IRON 5-IRON

JM

LAST SEASON

THIS

I'LL ALSO PROMISE THAT YOU WILL GO OVER A LOT FEWER GREENS THIS SEASON THAN YOU WERE SHORT OF LAST YEAR. HOW CAN I BE SO SURE?

AS EVERY TOUR PRO WILL CONFIRM, THE SINGLE GREATEST FAULT OF ALL AMATEURS WORLDWIDE IS UNDER-CLUBBING.

JUST CURING THAT WOULD SAVE MOST GOLFERS A HATFUL OF STROKES IN EVERY ROUND.

Go to Woods for Safer Shots

I SEE A LOT OF GOLFERS IN PRO-AMS WHOSE PRIDE KEEPS THEM USING LONG-IRONS WHEN THEY WOULD CERTAINLY PLAY A LOT BETTER BY REPLACING THEM WITH WOODS.

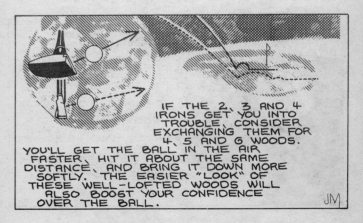

IF THE 2, 3 AND 4 IRONS GET YOU INTO TROUBLE, CONSIDER EXCHANGING THEM FOR 4, 5 AND 6 WOODS. YOU'LL GET THE BALL IN THE AIR FASTER, HIT IT ABOUT THE SAME DISTANCE, AND BRING IT DOWN MORE SOFTLY. THE EASIER "LOOK" OF THESE WELL-LOFTED WOODS WILL ALSO BOOST YOUR CONFIDENCE OVER THE BALL.

JM

N DOUBT AS TO WHETHER A FULL SWING WITH THE DRIVER MIGHT GET YOU IN TROUBLE FROM THE TEE?

ALWAYS GO TO THE THREE-WOOD IN SUCH CASES, RATHER THAN TRYING TO PLAY A LESS-THAN-FULL SHOT WITH THE DRIVER.

Reason? LETTING UP WITH THE DRIVER ALMOST ALWAYS LEADS TO EITHER QUITTING ON THE SHOT OR AN INVOLUNTARY ATTEMPT TO "STEER" THE BALL INTO POSITION, EITHER OF WHICH CAN CAUSE BIG PROBLEMS.

SO TAKE LESS CLUB AND SWING FULLY AND FREELY.

Weigh Up All the Risks

SOMETIMES IT'S DIFFICULT IN ASSESSING A TIGHT TEE SHOT TO DECIDE WHETHER TO SACRIFICE DISTANCE FOR ACCURACY.

I'VE FOUND THE FOLLOWING QUESTION HELPFUL IN SUCH CIRCUMSTANCES.

"IS THE POSSIBLE REWARD FOR EXTRA YARDAGE WORTH THE POTENTIAL RISK?"

I USUALLY FIND THE ONLY TIME I ANSWER "YES" IS WHEN I **MUST** HIT A DRIVER OFF THE TEE TO HAVE ANY CHANCE OF REACHING THE GREEN IN REGULATION.

NO. 7
375 YDS
PAR 4

Don't Try to Be a Hero

HANDICAP GOLFERS FREQUENTLY PERFORM A LOT WORSE IN STROKE-PLAY EVENTS THAN AT MATCH-PLAY.

THE CHIEF REASON IS TRYING TO HIT "HERO" SHOTS, RATHER THAN WORKING ALWAYS ON KEEPING THE BALL IN PLAY.

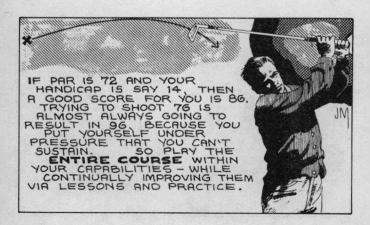

IF PAR IS 72 AND YOUR HANDICAP IS SAY 14, THEN A GOOD SCORE FOR YOU IS 86. TRYING TO SHOOT 76 IS ALMOST ALWAYS GOING TO RESULT IN 96, BECAUSE YOU PUT YOURSELF UNDER PRESSURE THAT YOU CAN'T SUSTAIN. SO PLAY THE **ENTIRE COURSE** WITHIN YOUR CAPABILITIES – WHILE CONTINUALLY IMPROVING THEM VIA LESSONS AND PRACTICE.

Tee Ball Up on Par Threes

OCCASIONALLY YOU'LL SEE A GOLFER PLAYING A PAR-THREE SIMPLY THROW THE BALL ON THE GROUND AND HIT AWAY.

IN MY BOOK HE'S MAKING THE GAME MUCH TOUGHER THAN IT NEED BE.

I ALWAYS TEE THE BALL ON A PEG WHEN THE RULES ALLOW, FIRST BECAUSE IT IMPROVES MY CHANCE OF MAKING SOLID CONTACT, AND SECONDLY BECAUSE IT REDUCES THE RISK OF GRASS GETTING BETWEEN CLUBFACE AND BALL AT IMPACT, THEREBY REDUCING BACKSPIN.

YOU SHOULD DO THE SAME.

NO. 7
165 YDS
PAR 3

JM

Be Ready When Your Turn Comes

SLOW PLAY IS A MAJOR PROBLEM IN GOLF TODAY, AND ONE THAT EVERY GOLFER SHOULD BE WORKING AT OUT OF CONSIDERATION FOR OTHERS, IF FOR NO OTHER REASON.

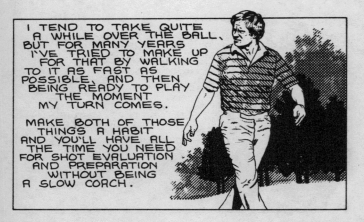

I TEND TO TAKE QUITE A WHILE OVER THE BALL, BUT FOR MANY YEARS I'VE TRIED TO MAKE UP FOR THAT BY WALKING TO IT AS FAST AS POSSIBLE, AND THEN BEING READY TO PLAY THE MOMENT MY TURN COMES.

MAKE BOTH OF THOSE THINGS A HABIT AND YOU'LL HAVE ALL THE TIME YOU NEED FOR SHOT EVALUATION AND PREPARATION WITHOUT BEING A SLOW COACH.

Know the Rules—They Can Help You

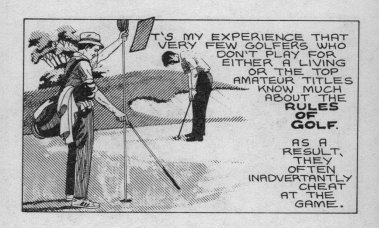

IT'S MY EXPERIENCE THAT VERY FEW GOLFERS WHO DON'T PLAY FOR EITHER A LIVING OR THE TOP AMATEUR TITLES KNOW MUCH ABOUT THE **RULES OF GOLF**.

AS A RESULT, THEY OFTEN INADVERTANTLY CHEAT AT THE GAME.

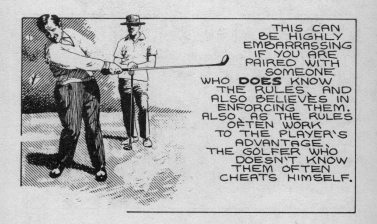

THIS CAN BE HIGHLY EMBARRASSING IF YOU ARE PAIRED WITH SOMEONE WHO **DOES** KNOW THE RULES, AND ALSO BELIEVES IN ENFORCING THEM. ALSO, AS THE RULES OFTEN WORK TO THE PLAYER'S ADVANTAGE, THE GOLFER WHO DOESN'T KNOW THEM OFTEN CHEATS HIMSELF.

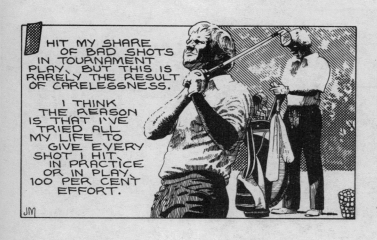

I HIT MY SHARE OF BAD SHOTS IN TOURNAMENT PLAY, BUT THIS IS RARELY THE RESULT OF CARELESSNESS.

I THINK THE REASON IS THAT I'VE TRIED ALL MY LIFE TO GIVE EVERY SHOT I HIT, IN PRACTICE OR IN PLAY, 100 PER CENT EFFORT.

MAN IS A CREATURE OF HABIT, THUS IF YOU HABITUALLY FAIL TO TRY YOUR HARDEST WHEN IT DOESN'T MATTER, THE CHANCES ARE YOU'LL ALSO GIVE LESS THAN YOUR BEST WHEN IT DOES.

TRYING 100 PER CENT ON **EVERY** SHOT IS FINE INSURANCE AGAINST THAT.

Part TWO

The Long Game

4

Preparing
to Swing

DO YOU WAIT UNTIL YOU'RE ACTUALLY OVER THE BALL BEFORE DECIDING EXACTLY WHERE YOU'RE TRYING TO HIT IT?

MANY HIGH HANDICAPPERS DO — WHICH IS ONE REASON THEY STAY HIGH HANDICAPPERS.

YOU CAN'T AIM CORRECTLY UNLESS YOU IDENTIFY A SPECIFIC TARGET TO ALIGN YOURSELF ON, SO PICK ONE OUT **BEFORE** YOU BEGIN TO SET-UP TO THE BALL.

MAKE IT A POINT IN THE BACKGROUND OR A MARK ON THE GROUND IF YOU'RE NOT GOING FOR THE PIN, BUT WHATEVER YOU CHOOSE — AIM <u>SPECIFICALLY</u>, NEVER VAGUELY.

Get the "Statics" Right

IF YOU HAVE NORMAL HEALTH AND STRENGTH, PLAY A COUPLE OF TIMES A WEEK OR MORE BUT CAN'T REGULARLY BREAK 90, YOUR PROBLEMS ALMOST CERTAINLY LIE IN YOUR GRIP AND SET-UP RATHER THAN IN THE WAY YOU SWING.

GETTING THESE "STATICS" RIGHT CAN BE UNCOMFORTABLE AND BORING COMPARED TO THE FUN OF WHACKING AT THE BALL. HOWEVER UNLESS YOU DO SO, YOU'RE ALWAYS GOING TO TAKE A LOT MORE WHACKS THAN YOU'D LIKE. TO FIND OUT HOW, GO SEE A GOOD TEACHING PRO — AND WATCH GOOD GOLFERS WHENEVER YOU CAN.

Form Grip When Clubhead Is Square

DON'T TAKE YOUR GRIP ON THE CLUB WHILE YOU'RE WAVING IT AROUND IN THE AIR — A COMMON FAULT OF POOR PLAYERS.

EXACT ALIGNMENT OF THE HANDS TO THE CLUBFACE AND OF THE CLUBFACE TO THE TARGET IS VITAL, AND THE ONLY WAY YOU CAN DO THAT IS WHEN THE CLUBHEAD IS BEHIND THE BALL.

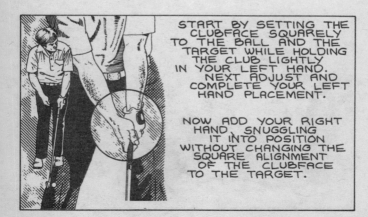

START BY SETTING THE CLUBFACE SQUARELY TO THE BALL AND THE TARGET WHILE HOLDING THE CLUB LIGHTLY IN YOUR LEFT HAND. NEXT ADJUST AND COMPLETE YOUR LEFT HAND PLACEMENT.

NOW ADD YOUR RIGHT HAND, SNUGGLING IT INTO POSITION WITHOUT CHANGING THE SQUARE ALIGNMENT OF THE CLUBFACE TO THE TARGET.

Make Your Hands a Single Unit

MANY BEGINNERS FIND IT DIFFICULT TO KEEP THEIR HANDS TOGETHER AND WORKING AS A SINGLE UNIT THROUGHOUT THE SWING.

LETTING THE HANDS SEPARATE OR WORK INDEPENDENTLY OF EACH OTHER IS ALSO RESPONSIBLE FOR MUCH POOR PLAY AMONG ESTABLISHED GOLFERS.

JM

I BELIEVE THE INTERLOCKING GRIP, THE ONE I'VE ALWAYS USED, OFFERS THE BEST SOLUTION TO THIS PROBLEM. WHEN IT IS PROPERLY ASSEMBLED AS SEEN HERE, HAND SEPARATION OR INDEPENDENT MOTION BECOME ALMOST IMPOSSIBLE. HOWEVER, GIVE YOURSELF PLENTY OF PRACTICE TIME TO GET USED TO THE NEW "FEEL" IF YOU DECIDE TO TRY IT.

Grip with Left Hand First

QUITE A FEW GOLFERS SEEM TO FIND DIFFICULTY IN MAINTAINING A SQUARE CLUBFACE AS THEY SET-UP TO THE BALL.

ONE WAY TO SOLVE THE PROBLEM IS TO GRIP WITH THE **LEFT HAND** ONLY UNTIL THE ADDRESS IS COMPLETED. THEN EASE THE RIGHT HAND GENTLY INTO POSITION.

AN EXTRA BENEFIT OF THIS TECHNIQUE IS THAT IT HELPS IN SETTING THE RIGHT SIDE PROPERLY "UNDER" THE LEFT SIDE AT ADDRESS — A PARTICULARLY IMPORTANT POSTURAL FACTOR FOR SLICERS AND PULLERS.

Grip Lightly to Avoid Misalignment

A LOT OF ERRANT SHOTS ARE THE RESULT OF INVOLUNTARILY MISALIGNING THE CLUBFACE, RELATIVE TO THE TARGET, AT SOME POINT IN SETTING-UP TO THE BALL.

IT'S VERY EASY TO DO THIS WITH THE RIGHT HAND PARTICULARLY, AND ESPECIALLY IF YOU TEND TO "GRAB" THE CLUB WITH IT.

TO AVOID THIS SMALL BUT COSTLY FAULT, TRY HOLDING VERY LIGHTLY AS YOU SET-UP TO THE BALL, THEN FIRM UP YOUR GRIP TO THE CORRECT TAKEAWAY PRESSURE JUST BEFORE BEGINNING THE BACKSWING.

AND TRY TO SUSTAIN AN EVEN PRESSURE RIGHT ON UP TO THE TOP — DON'T "GRAB."

Try This for an Even Grip Pressure

TO ENSURE AN EVENLY SECURE GRIP PRESSURE THROUGHOUT THE SWING, BEGIN BY HOLDING THE CLUB FAIRLY EASILY AS YOU COMPLETE YOUR ADDRESS POSITION. THEN FIRM UP YOUR HANDS TO YOUR IDEAL SWING PRESSURE JUST BEFORE STARTING BACK.

JM

IF YOU HAVE PROBLEMS MAINTAINING THE FIRMNESS AT THE TOP, PRACTICE HITTING SHOTS WHILE CONSCIOUSLY SNUGGLING THE PAD OF YOUR RIGHT THUMB AGAINST THE TOP OF YOUR LEFT THUMB. PREVENT GAPS BETWEEN THESE TWO AREAS AND IT IS ALMOST IMPOSSIBLE TO LET GO OF THE CLUB.

"Grip-Press" for Smooth Takeaway

MOST GOLFERS KNOW THE IMPORTANCE OF STARTING THE CLUB AWAY FROM THE BALL SMOOTHLY, BUT MANY HAVE TROUBLE DOING SO.

HERE'S A TIP THAT MIGHT HELP.

HOLD THE CLUB FAIRLY LIGHTLY AS YOU FINALIZE YOUR SET-UP TO THE BALL, THEN FIRM UP YOUR HANDS AS THE LAST ACTION BEFORE YOU START THE CLUBHEAD BACK.

I'VE USED THIS "**GRIP-PRESS**" FOR YEARS AS AN AID TO A SMOOTH TAKEAWAY, AND IT COULD HELP YOUR GAME TOO.

JM

Check Grip Pressure After Impact

IF YOU'RE HITTING THE BALL SOLIDLY BUT NOT AS ACCURATELY AS USUAL, CHECK YOUR GRIP PRESSURE <u>AFTER</u> IMPACT.

LOOSENING THE HANDS THROUGH THE IMPACT AREA — OFTEN INVOLUNTARILY — IS A COMMON BUT LITTLE-RECOGNIZED CAUSE OF "SPRAYING."

I FIRM UP MY HANDS AS PART OF MY FORWARD-PRESS, THEN TRY TO MAINTAIN AN <u>EVEN PRESSURE</u> RIGHT THROUGH TO THE END OF THE <u>FOLLOW-THROUGH.</u>

CONSCIOUSLY BEING FIRM THROUGH IMPACT WILL OFTEN ADD BOTH CRISPNESS AND CONTROL TO YOUR SHOTS.

FIRM

Check Lower Hand for Unified Action

SEEMINGLY SMALL ADJUSTMENTS CAN SOMETIMES BRING BIG BENEFITS AT GOLF.

FOR INSTANCE, IF YOU HAVE DIFFICULTY WORKING YOUR HANDS AS A SINGLE UNIT DURING THE SWING, CHECK THE SNUGNESS OF THE FINGERS OF YOUR LOWER HAND.

"TRIGGERING" THE CLUB WITH THE FOREFINGER SEEMS TO COME NATURALLY TO MANY GOLFERS.

HOWEVER, IT CREATES A GAP BETWEEN THE FOREFINGER AND THE MIDDLE FINGER THAT IN MY CASE MAKES IT HARDER TO UNIFY MY HAND ACTION.

COULD BE THIS IS TRUE FOR YOU, TOO.

Take a Natural Stance

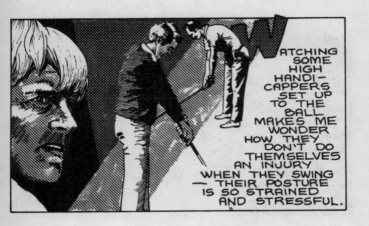

WATCHING SOME HIGH HANDI-CAPPERS SET UP TO THE BALL MAKES ME WONDER HOW THEY DON'T DO THEMSELVES AN INJURY WHEN THEY SWING — THEIR POSTURE IS SO STRAINED AND STRESSFUL.

THE FOUR PRINCIPLES OF GOOD POSTURE ARE: BEND AT THE WAIST; KEEP THE BACK AS STRAIGHT AS COMFORTABLY POSSIBLE; LET THE ARMS HANG FREELY AND EASILY; AND SLIGHTLY FLEX THE KNEES. WITHIN THOSE SIMPLE GUIDELINES IT PAYS TO BE AS NATURAL AS POSSIBLE WHEN TAKING YOUR STANCE AT THE BALL.

Don't Contort Your Body at Address

FORCE SOME PART OF YOUR BODY INTO A CONTRIVED POSITION AT ADDRESS AND CHANCES ARE IT WILL REVERT TO NATURE ONCE YOU START MOVING, WITH NEGATIVE EFFECT ON YOUR SHOTS.

JM

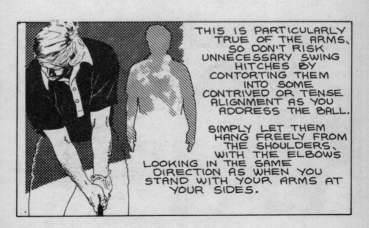

THIS IS PARTICULARLY TRUE OF THE ARMS, SO DON'T RISK UNNECESSARY SWING HITCHES BY CONTORTING THEM INTO SOME CONTRIVED OR TENSE ALIGNMENT AS YOU ADDRESS THE BALL.

SIMPLY LET THEM HANG FREELY FROM THE SHOULDERS, WITH THE ELBOWS LOOKING IN THE SAME DIRECTION AS WHEN YOU STAND WITH YOUR ARMS AT YOUR SIDES.

Never Start from Immobile Position

THE WORST WAY TO START YOUR GOLF SWING IS FROM A TOTALLY IMMOBILE POSITION, SO DEVELOP YOURSELF AN EFFECTIVE SWING "TRIGGER."

THIS COULD BE A FORWARD PRESS OF THE HANDS AND ARMS, OR A TARGETWARD SHIFT OF THE KNEES, OR ANY **SMALL** MOTION THAT ENABLES YOU TO START THE CLUB BACK FLUIDLY.

MY "TRIGGER" IS A FIRMING OF THE GRIP COMBINED WITH A SWIVELING OF THE CHIN AWAY FROM THE TARGET TO ALLOW THE FULLEST POSSIBLE COILING OF MY SHOULDERS GOING BACK. EXPERIMENT IN PRACTICE TO DETERMINE WHAT WORKS BEST FOR YOU, THEN "GROOVE" YOUR OWN PERSONAL TRIGGER UNTIL YOU DO IT SUBCONSCIOUSLY ON EVERY SHOT.

Begin the Swing Deliberately

MOST GOLFERS KNOW THAT THE PACE AT WHICH THEY START THE CLUB BACK FROM THE BALL IS CRITICAL TO THE SUCCESS OF THE SHOT. BUT MANY STILL HAVE TROUBLE ACHIEVING A CONSISTENTLY SMOOTH MOTION.

THE THOUGHT THAT HELPS ME MOST IN BEGINNING THE BACKSWING IS "DELIBERATENESS."

TO PICTURE THAT PACE, COMPARE IT TO GETTING A CAR ROLLING AS SMOOTHLY AS POSSIBLE, WITH A GENTLE STARTING MOTION FOLLOWED BY A GRADUAL BUILD-UP IN ACCELERATION.

CHECK YOUR BALL POSITION AT ADDRESS ANY TIME YOUR SHOTS START CURVING BADLY RIGHT OR LEFT.

SETTING THE BALL TOO FAR FORWARD OR BACK IN RELATION TO YOUR FEET COULD BE THE CAUSE OF THE PROBLEM.

WITH THE BALL TOO FAR FORWARD, YOU ARE FORCED TO SWING ACROSS IT FROM OUT TO IN, AS DIAGRAM 1 SHOWS HERE.

CONVERSELY, AS WE SEE IN DIAGRAM 2, POSITIONING THE BALL TOO FAR BACK CAUSES THE CLUB TO MEET IT WHILE SWINGING FROM IN TO OUT.

5

Avoiding
Head Movement

Make "Head Still" No. 1 Rule

WE'VE SAID IT BEFORE, BUT IT'S WORTH SAYING AGAIN: KEEPING THE **HEAD STILL** IS THE <u>NO. 1 FUNDAMENTAL OF GOLF.</u>

BECAUSE IT'S SO DIFFICULT TO SELF-DIAGNOSE, IT'S WORTH HAVING YOUR PRO OR A PAL CHECK YOU OUT PERIODICALLY.

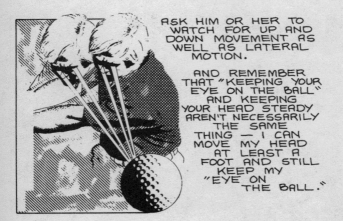

ASK HIM OR HER TO WATCH FOR UP AND DOWN MOVEMENT AS WELL AS LATERAL MOTION.

AND REMEMBER THAT "KEEPING YOUR EYE ON THE BALL" AND KEEPING YOUR HEAD STEADY AREN'T NECESSARILY THE SAME THING — I CAN MOVE MY HEAD AT LEAST A FOOT AND STILL KEEP MY "EYE ON THE BALL."

Watch Shadow to Check Movement

PRONOUNCED HEAD MOVEMENT AT ANY POINT FROM TAKEAWAY TO IMPACT IS A SURE SHOT-WRECKER.

BEST WAY TO CHECK THAT YOURS IS STAYING STEADY IS WITH THE HELP OF YOUR PRO OR A GOLFING FRIEND.

WHEN THAT'S IMPRACTICAL, YOU CAN GET A PRETTY GOOD READING SIMPLY BY PRACTICE SWINGING WITH THE SUN DIRECTLY BEHIND YOU.

HIT AT A TEE PEG OR A WEED, WATCHING YOUR SHADOW CAREFULLY WHILE DOING SO.

JM

Try Checking Head Sway This Way

MANY GOLFERS WHO MOVE THEIR HEADS DURING THE SWING DON'T BELIEVE THEY

ARE DOING SO BECAUSE THEY CAN'T ACTUALLY FEEL OR SENSE IT HAPPENING.

IF YOU'D LIKE TO TAKE THE ULTIMATE TEST REGARDING HEAD MOVEMENT, HAVE SOMEONE GRAB YOUR HAIR WHILE STANDING IN FRONT OF YOU AS YOU SWING WITH A SHORT OR MEDIUM IRON.

THE FEELING IN YOUR SCALP WILL GIVE YOU A VERY CONCLUSIVE ANSWER!

Beware Up-and-Down Movement, Too

A STEADY HEAD IS THE SINGLE MOST IMPORTANT FACTOR IN GOLF — AN **ABSOLUTE MUST**.

MOST GOLFERS KNOW AND TRY TO AVOID THE DESTRUCTIVE EFFECTS OF SIDE-TO-SIDE MOVEMENT.

WHAT MANY OVERLOOK ARE THE EQUALLY RUINOUS RESULTS OF UP-AND-DOWN MOVEMENT.

LIFT OR LOWER YOUR HEAD AT ANY POINT IN THE SWING AND YOU CHANGE IT'S ARC.

SO IF YOU TEND EITHER TO TOP SHOTS OR HIT A LOT OF THEM "FAT," HAVE SOMEONE CHECK OUT HOW YOUR HEAD IS BEHAVING.

IF IT'S WOBBLING IN ANY DIRECTION, MAKE KEEPING IT STEADY YOUR NO. 1 CONSCIOUS SWING THOUGHT FOR THE MONTH.

HERE'S A TIP TO HELP YOU LEARN TO KEEP YOUR HEAD STEADY THROUGHOUT THE SWING — AN ABSOLUTE "MUST" FOR PLAYING UP TO YOUR FULL POTENTIAL.

IT WILL ALSO, INCIDENTALLY, IMPROVE YOUR FOOTWORK.

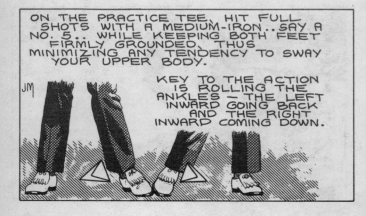

ON THE PRACTICE TEE, HIT FULL SHOTS WITH A MEDIUM-IRON..SAY A NO. 5.. WHILE KEEPING BOTH FEET FIRMLY GROUNDED, THUS MINIMIZING ANY TENDENCY TO SWAY YOUR UPPER BODY.

JM

KEY TO THE ACTION IS ROLLING THE ANKLES — THE LEFT INWARD GOING BACK AND THE RIGHT INWARD COMING DOWN.

Think "Head Still"!

keep your head still IS AN AGE-OLD GOLFING MAXIM, BUT THE FACT IS IT RARELY HAPPENS EVEN IN THE FINEST SWINGS. PHOTOGRAPHY PROVES THAT GOOD PLAYERS' HEADS USUALLY MOVE A LITTLE BACK AND DOWN AS THEY HIT THROUGH THE BALL.

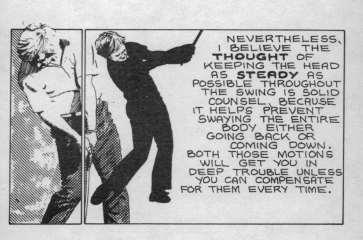

NEVERTHELESS, I BELIEVE THE **THOUGHT** OF KEEPING THE HEAD AS **STEADY** AS POSSIBLE THROUGHOUT THE SWING IS SOLID COUNSEL, BECAUSE IT HELPS PREVENT SWAYING THE ENTIRE BODY EITHER GOING BACK OR COMING DOWN. BOTH THOSE MOTIONS WILL GET YOU IN DEEP TROUBLE UNLESS YOU CAN COMPENSATE FOR THEM EVERY TIME.

6

Improving Your Tempo

Don't Let "Grabbing" Wreck Your Rhythm

THE MORE RHYTHMICAL YOUR GOLF SWING, THE BETTER IT WILL WORK.

"GRABBING" THE CLUB WITH THE HANDS AT SOME POINT IN THE BACKSWING IS A SURE RHYTHM-WRECKER.

OFTEN THIS ACTION IS INVOLUNTARY. IF YOU SUSPECT YOU ARE DOING IT, TRY MAKING A **CONSCIOUS** EFFORT ON EVERY SWING TO HOLD THE CLUB FIRMLY BUT NOT TIGHTLY AT ADDRESS, THEN MAINTAIN THE EXACT SAME PRESSURE FROM THERE ON THROUGH. IF YOUR SWING BEGINS TO FEEL SMOOTHER, YOU CAN BE SURE YOU'VE BEEN A "GRABBER."

Use Big Muscles to Smooth Tempo

GOT TIMING PROBLEMS??

THE BIGGER THE MUSCLE-GROUPS YOU USE IN EVERYDAY ACTIONS, THE MORE DELIBERATELY AND THUS THE MORE SMOOTHLY YOU'LL TEND TO MOVE.

SAME IN GOLF.

TO IMPROVE YOUR TEMPO AND RHYTHM, TRY MOTIVATING THE CLUB MORE WITH YOUR BODY AND LESS WITH YOUR HANDS, WRISTS AND ARMS.

WORK PARTICULARLY ON A FULL UPPER TORSO TURN GOING BACK, AND FULL HIP CLEARANCE ON THE WAY TO AND THROUGH THE BALL.

Swing in "Slow Motion" to Improve Form

IF YOU'VE TRIED EVERYTHING ELSE TO ELIMINATE A SWING FLAW AND HAVEN'T SUCCEEDED, TRY SLOWING DOWN YOUR TEMPO.

ON SECOND THOUGHTS, TRY THIS FIRST BECAUSE IT MIGHT SAVE YOU A GREAT DEAL OF TIME AND EFFORT.

BY PLAYING IN EFFECT IN SLOW MOTION, YOU GIVE YOURSELF TIME TO REALLY **FEEL** WHAT YOU ARE DOING AS YOU EXECUTE THE SWING.

VERY OFTEN THAT ALONE WILL TELL YOU HOW TO GO ABOUT CORRECTING IT — PLUS GIVING YOU THE TIME TO DO SO.

SLOW TEMPO

Lengthen Swing to Slow It Down

IF YOU THINK YOU'D PLAY BETTER WITH A SLOWER TEMPO, TRY LENGTHENING YOUR SWING BY INCREASING YOUR SHOULDER TURN AND ARM EXTENSION.

JM

THE FULLER THE SWING, THE LONGER IT TAKES TO EXECUTE — WHICH WILL AUTOMATICALLY SLOW DOWN YOUR OVERALL TEMPO.

KEY IS TO **COIL** AND **EXTEND** MORE, RATHER THAN SIMPLY BENDING YOUR LEFT ARM OR RELAXING YOUR GRIP TO LET THE CLUB GO BACK FARTHER.

PROPERLY TIMING THE TRANSITION FROM BACKSWING TO THROUGH-SWING IS ONE OF GOLF'S TOUGHEST CHALLENGES.

MOST GOLFERS TEND TO RUSH THE CHANGEOVER CAUSING THEM TO SWING "OVER AND OUT" WITH THEIR SHOULDERS.

TO PREVENT THIS, PRACTICE ONE OF MY KEY SWING THOUGHTS, WHICH IS:

"SWING THE HANDS AND ARMS DOWN AT THE SAME **DELIBERATE** PACE YOU SWUNG THEM STARTING BACK."

THE MOVEMENT WILL ACTUALLY BE FASTER THAN YOUR STARTING-BACK MOTION, BUT THE **THOUGHT** OF BEING EQUALLY DELIBERATE WILL DEFINITELY HELP YOU ACHIEVE PROPER TIMING.

Try This Drill for Better Timing

TIMING YOUR SHOTS POORLY?

OUT OF BALANCE AT IMPACT?

HIT SOME SHOTS WITH YOUR FEET **TOGETHER**

ACTUALLY <u>TOUCHING AT THE HEELS</u>

JM

USE A FIVE- OR SIX-IRON, AND BUILD UP GRADUALLY FROM A HALF- TO A THREE-QUARTER SWING.

REGULAR PRACTICE LIKE THIS WILL DO WONDERS FOR YOUR TEMPO AND BALANCE — AND TEACH YOU GOOD <u>HAND ACTION</u> AS WELL.

7

Building a Better Swing

Check These Fundamentals

BEWARE OF OVER-EXPERIMENTING ANY TIME YOUR GAME GOES SOUR.

GIMMICKS MAY WORK FOR SHORT PERIODS, BUT IN THE LONG RUN THERE IS NO SUBSTITUTE FOR FUNDAMENTALS.

JM

IF YOU'RE PLAYING CONSISTENTLY POORLY, CHECK IN ORDER — PREFERABLY WITH THE HELP OF A TEACHING PROFESSIONAL — YOUR GRIP, YOUR AIM, YOUR ALIGNMENT, AND YOUR POSTURE. USUALLY THE FAULT WILL LIE, AT **ROOT**, IN ONE OF THOSE AREAS. ONLY AFTER YOU'VE SATISFIED YOURSELF THAT IT DOESN'T SHOULD YOU CONSIDER ACTUAL SWING CHANGES.

Develop One Basic Swing

BEGINNERS AND SELF-TAUGHT GOLFERS OFTEN SEEM TO THINK THAT, BECAUSE THEIR GOLF CLUBS VARY IN LENGTH AND HEAD CONFIGURATION, EACH OF THEM MUST BE SWUNG DIFFERENTLY. THAT'S 100% THE WRONG APPROACH.

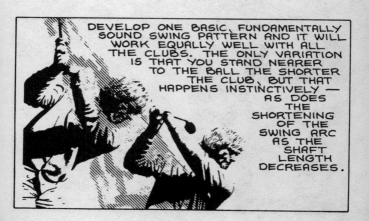

DEVELOP ONE BASIC, FUNDAMENTALLY SOUND SWING PATTERN AND IT WILL WORK EQUALLY WELL WITH ALL THE CLUBS. THE ONLY VARIATION IS THAT YOU STAND NEARER TO THE BALL THE SHORTER THE CLUB, BUT THAT HAPPENS INSTINCTIVELY — AS DOES THE SHORTENING OF THE SWING ARC AS THE SHAFT LENGTH DECREASES.

Cock Chin for a Complete Backswing

COMING "OVER" OR "OFF" THE BALL IN THE DOWNSWING??

THOSE ARE VERY COMMON FAULTS, AND FREQUENTLY THEIR CAUSE IS NOTHING MORE COMPLICATED THAN AN INCOMPLETE BODY TURN ON THE BACKSWING.

HERE'S A TIP THAT WILL HELP ANYONE WHO TENDS TO START DOWN BEFORE THEY'VE FINISHED GOING BACK.

AS YOU BEGIN THE BACKSWING, SIMPLY TURN YOUR CHIN A FEW DEGREES TO THE RIGHT.

YOU'LL FIND THIS ACTION, COMMON TO MANY TOUR PLAYERS, INCLUDING ME, ALLOWS YOU A LOT MORE ROOM TO FULLY WIND UP THOSE SHOULDERS AND HIPS.

Stay "Soft" in Your Trailing Hand

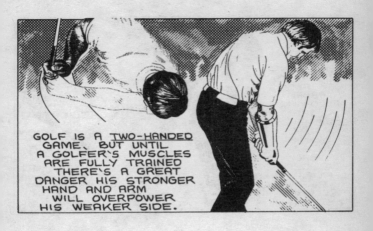

GOLF IS A <u>TWO-HANDED</u> GAME, BUT UNTIL A GOLFER'S MUSCLES ARE FULLY TRAINED THERE'S A GREAT DANGER HIS STRONGER HAND AND ARM WILL OVERPOWER HIS WEAKER SIDE.

WAY TO OVERCOME THIS IS TO ESTABLISH A SENSATION OF "SOFTNESS" IN THE TRAILING HAND AND ARM AT ADDRESS, THEN CONSCIOUSLY TRY TO KEEP THEM PASSIVE THROUGHOUT THE SWING. LET THEM JUST "GO ALONG FOR THE RIDE" MOST OF THE TIME, AND THEY'LL AUTOMATICALLY DO THEIR JOB IN THE HITTING AREA IN RESPONSE TO CENTRIFUGAL FORCE.

JM

Don't Let the Clubhead Lag

ALL KINDS OF MISHITS CAN RESULT FROM ALLOWING THE CLUBHEAD TO **LAG** BEHIND THE HANDS STARTING BACK, BREAKING THE IDEAL STRAIGHT LEFT ARM/CLUBSHAFT TAKEAWAY RELATIONSHIP.

OVERLY RELAXED WRISTS CAN CAUSE THIS FAULT, SO BE SURE YOU'RE FIRM HERE AS THE BACKSWING MOTION BEGINS.

CHECK HOW YOU GROUND THE CLUB, ALSO, BECAUSE STUBBING THE CLUB THROUGH PRESSING DOWN TOO FIRMLY AT ADDRESS CAN ALSO CAUSE A SHOT-WRECKING LAG.

Keep Hands Passive for Fuller Turn

HAVE PROBLEMS MAKING A GOOD UPPER BODY TURN?

KEEPING YOUR HANDS AND WRISTS PASSIVE UNTIL THE CLUB HAS SWUNG BEYOND HIP HEIGHT GOING BACK WILL HELP YOU TO EXTEND YOUR ARMS AND COIL YOUR SHOULDERS FULLY.

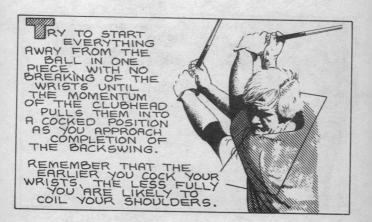

TRY TO START EVERYTHING AWAY FROM THE BALL IN ONE PIECE, WITH NO BREAKING OF THE WRISTS UNTIL THE MOMENTUM OF THE CLUBHEAD PULLS THEM INTO A COCKED POSITION AS YOU APPROACH COMPLETION OF THE BACKSWING.

REMEMBER THAT THE EARLIER YOU COCK YOUR WRISTS, THE LESS FULLY YOU ARE LIKELY TO COIL YOUR SHOULDERS.

Keep Left Arm Firmly Extended

ONE OF THE BIGGEST FAULTS OF BEGINNERS AND POOR PLAYERS IS BENDING THE LEFT ARM DURING THE BACKSWING, CAUSING LOSS OF BOTH CONTROL AND POWER.

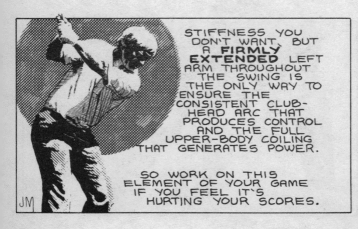

STIFFNESS YOU DON'T WANT, BUT A **FIRMLY EXTENDED** LEFT ARM THROUGHOUT THE SWING IS THE ONLY WAY TO ENSURE THE CONSISTENT CLUB-HEAD ARC THAT PRODUCES CONTROL AND THE FULL UPPER-BODY COILING THAT GENERATES POWER.

SO WORK ON THIS ELEMENT OF YOUR GAME IF YOU FEEL IT'S HURTING YOUR SCORES.

Keep Your Right Knee Flexed

ANY TIME YOUR RIGHT KNEE STRAIGHTENS ON THE BACKSWING, YOU DIMINISH DISTANCE-PRODUCING TORQUE AND RISK SWINGING "OVER THE TOP."

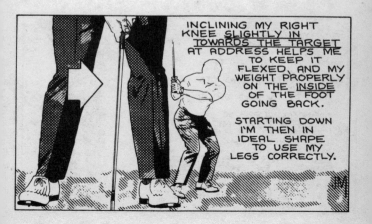

INCLINING MY RIGHT KNEE SLIGHTLY IN TOWARDS THE TARGET AT ADDRESS HELPS ME TO KEEP IT FLEXED, AND MY WEIGHT PROPERLY ON THE INSIDE OF THE FOOT GOING BACK.

STARTING DOWN I'M THEN IN IDEAL SHAPE TO USE MY LEGS CORRECTLY.

Check Your Backswing Hip Turn

"SPINNING OUT?"

COMING "OVER THE BALL?"

CHECK HOW YOUR HIPS ARE WORKING IN THE BACKSWING --- ESPECIALLY IF YOUR LEGS AREN'T PARTICULARLY STRONG OR WELL-CONDITIONED.

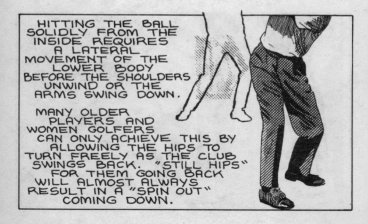

HITTING THE BALL SOLIDLY FROM THE INSIDE REQUIRES A LATERAL MOVEMENT OF THE LOWER BODY BEFORE THE SHOULDERS UNWIND OR THE ARMS SWING DOWN.

MANY OLDER PLAYERS AND WOMEN GOLFERS CAN ONLY ACHIEVE THIS BY ALLOWING THE HIPS TO TURN FREELY AS THE CLUB SWINGS BACK. "STILL HIPS" FOR THEM GOING BACK WILL ALMOST ALWAYS RESULT IN A "SPIN OUT" COMING DOWN.

Try "Long Left Thumb" for Over-Wristiness

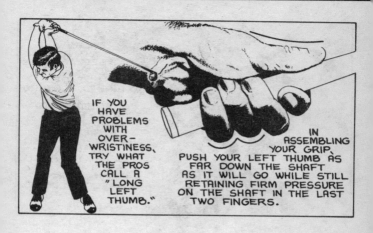

IF YOU HAVE PROBLEMS WITH OVER-WRISTINESS, TRY WHAT THE PROS CALL A "LONG LEFT THUMB."

IN ASSEMBLING YOUR GRIP, PUSH YOUR LEFT THUMB AS FAR DOWN THE SHAFT AS IT WILL GO WHILE STILL RETAINING FIRM PRESSURE ON THE SHAFT IN THE LAST TWO FINGERS.

THIS WILL HAVE THE EFFECT OF SETTING THE CLUB MORE IN THE PALM OF THE LEFT HAND, WHICH WILL HELP TO FIRM UP YOUR HAND AND WRIST ACTION THROUGHOUT THE SWING.

Cultivate Feeling of "Coiled Strength"

BACKSWING HIP ACTION SEEMS TO TROUBLE A LOT OF WEEKEND PLAYERS.

FEELING TO STRIVE FOR IS THAT THE RIGHT SIDE IS NEITHER LOCKED TIGHT NOR LOOSELY RELAXED AS THE BACKSWING IS COMPLETED.

LEFT HIP FOR A LEFTY

A SENSATION OF **COILED STRENGTH** IS MY OBJECTIVE.

THE SENSATION IS NOT OF TENSION BUT OF <u>SPRINGINESS</u> — GIVING ME THE CAPABILITY TO MOVE MY LEGS AND HIPS QUICKLY BUT SMOOTHLY INTO THE DOWNSWING.

Learn to Stay Behind the Ball

MOVE YOUR BODY FORWARD OF ITS ADDRESS POSITION DURING THE SWING AND YOU CAN HIT EVERY TYPE OF CROOKED SHOT IN THE BOOK.

AN OVER-VIOLENT EFFORT TO SHIFT THE WEIGHT TO THE LEFT SIDE CAN CAUSE THE ENTIRE BODY TO MOVE FORWARD. SO CAN TOO MUCH LATERAL HIP SLIDE COMING DOWN AND THROUGH, AS OPPOSED TO A SLIDE-AND-TURN HIP ACTION.

SIMPLE WAY TO BE SURE OF STAYING BEHIND THE BALL, HOWEVER, IS TO KEEP YOUR HEAD STEADY. DO THAT AND IT'S IMPOSSIBLE TO MOVE YOUR UPPER HALF FORWARD ALONG WITH YOUR LOWER HALF.

Trust Your Centrifugal Force

Some golfers fail to initiate and lead the downswing with their legs and hips because of fear that their hands and wrists won't get the clubhead to the ball in time to make flush contact.

Don't fall into that trap. Correct lower-body action coming down builds up such massive centrifugal force in the clubhead that your hands and wrists will react to it reflexively.

In fact, the "later" you can make the release the better — so long as you DO release fully when the time comes.

Angle Left Foot for Easier Unwinding

HAVE TROUBLE BEGINNING THE DOWNSWING WITH YOUR LEGS AND HIPS??

CHECK YOUR LEFT FOOT POSITIONING AT ADDRESS, BECAUSE A SLIGHT CHANGE HERE COULD SOLVE THE PROBLEM.

FOR MOST GOLFERS, THE MORE TOWARDS THE TARGET THE LEFT FOOT IS ANGLED AT ADDRESS, THE EASIER IT BECOMES TO UNWIND THE LOWER BODY THROUGHOUT THE DOWNSWING.

TRY THIS ON THE PRACTICE TEE, ESPECIALLY IF YOU'VE HABITUALLY SET UP WITH YOUR LEAD FOOT SET PRETTY MUCH SQUARE.

Use Legs Properly Coming Down

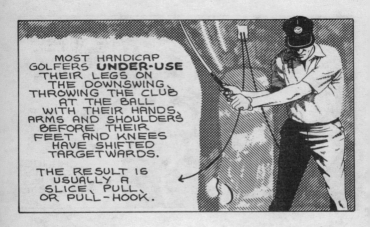

MOST HANDICAP GOLFERS **UNDER-USE** THEIR LEGS ON THE DOWNSWING, THROWING THE CLUB AT THE BALL WITH THEIR HANDS, ARMS AND SHOULDERS BEFORE THEIR FEET AND KNEES HAVE SHIFTED TARGETWARDS.

THE RESULT IS USUALLY A SLICE, PULL, OR PULL-HOOK.

HOWEVER, IT'S ALSO POSSIBLE TO **OVER-USE** THE LEGS, MOVING THE LOWER HALF OF THE BODY SO FAR AND SO VIOLENTLY TARGETWARDS THAT THERE IS NO TIME TO UNWIND THE HIPS TO MAKE ROOM FOR THE HANDS AND ARMS TO SWING FREELY THROUGH ALONG THE TARGET LINE.

HOOKING, PUSHING AND PUSH-SLICING ARE SIGNS OF THIS FAULT.

Feel Firm in Your Left Side

BOTH ACCURACY AND POWER ARE LOST BY CRUMPLING OR COLLAPSING THE LEFT SIDE THROUGH IMPACT — A COMMON EVENT IN HIGH-HANDICAP PLAY.

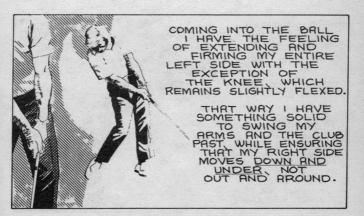

COMING INTO THE BALL I HAVE THE FEELING OF EXTENDING AND FIRMING MY ENTIRE LEFT SIDE WITH THE EXCEPTION OF THE KNEE, WHICH REMAINS SLIGHTLY FLEXED.

THAT WAY I HAVE SOMETHING SOLID TO SWING MY ARMS AND THE CLUB PAST, WHILE ENSURING THAT MY RIGHT SIDE MOVES DOWN AND UNDER, NOT OUT AND AROUND.

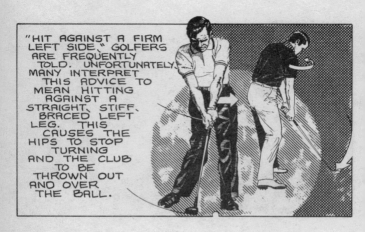

"HIT AGAINST A FIRM LEFT SIDE," GOLFERS ARE FREQUENTLY TOLD. UNFORTUNATELY, MANY INTERPRET THIS ADVICE TO MEAN HITTING AGAINST A STRAIGHT, STIFF, BRACED LEFT LEG. THIS CAUSES THE HIPS TO STOP TURNING AND THE CLUB TO BE THROWN OUT AND OVER THE BALL.

BY ALL MEANS STRETCH AND EXTEND YOUR LEFT SIDE THROUGH THE BALL, BUT DO IT WITH A SLIGHT **FLEX** IN THE LEFT KNEE.

THAT WAY YOUR HIPS CAN KEEP TURNING THROUGH THE SHOT, WHICH ALLOWS YOUR RIGHT SHOULDER TO SWING DOWN AND UNDER, NOT OUT AND AROUND.

Clear Hips on Through-Swing

GIVEN THAT YOU'VE MADE A GOOD, FULL BACKSWING TURN, NEVER RESTRICT THE UNWINDING OF THE HIPS AS THE THROUGH-SWING PROGRESSES.

FAILURE TO DO SO WILL RESULT IN THE FAULTS SHOWN HERE — "BLOCKING" AND/OR COLLAPSING THE LEFT ARM THROUGH IMPACT.

CLEARING THE HIPS COMING DOWN IS THE ONLY WAY TO MAKE ROOM FOR YOUR ARMS TO SWING FREELY PAST YOUR BODY AND ON OUT TOWARDS THE TARGET.

SO WIND UP FULLY ON THE BACKSWING, THEN LET THOSE HIPS UNWIND AS YOUR LEGS MOVE YOU INTO THE BALL.

Practice "Staying Down"

ANXIETY CAUSES MANY GOLFERS TO RAISE UP TOO QUICKLY AS THEY HIT THE BALL. SO DOES POOR SWING FORM. ONE ANTIDOTE TO BOTH IS TO PRACTICE DELIBERATELY "STAYING DOWN" LONGER THROUGH THE IMPACT AREA.

EASIEST WAY I KNOW TO ACHIEVE THIS IS TO TRY TO KEEP THE FOLLOW-THROUGH AS LOW AS POSSIBLE FOR AS LONG AS POSSIBLE. A FEELING OF EXTENDING THE ARMS AS FAR AS THEY'LL GO AFTER THE HIT IS ALSO HELPFUL.

SO IS KEEPING THE LEFT KNEE SLIGHTLY FLEXED THROUGH IMPACT.

Try This for Truer Swinging Motion

MANY HIGH-HANDICAPPERS WOULD IMPROVE ENORMOUSLY SIMPLY BY CONSCIOUSLY THINKING ON EVERY SHOT OF SWINGING <u>THROUGH</u> RATHER THAN TO THE BALL.

ONE USEFUL MENTAL PICTURE IS SIMPLY OF THE BALL ACCIDENTALLY HAPPENING TO BE ON THE CLUBHEAD PATH.

ANOTHER IS THINKING OF SWEEPING THE CLUB AS SMOOTHLY AS POSSIBLE THROUGH AN ARC FROM THREE OR FOUR FEET BEHIND THE BALL TO THREE OR FOUR FEET BEYOND IT.

Beware Letting Go of Club

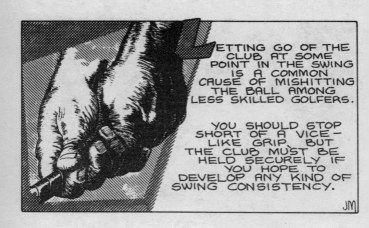

LETTING GO OF THE CLUB AT SOME POINT IN THE SWING IS A COMMON CAUSE OF MISHITTING THE BALL AMONG LESS SKILLED GOLFERS.

YOU SHOULD STOP SHORT OF A VICE-LIKE GRIP, BUT THE CLUB MUST BE HELD SECURELY IF YOU HOPE TO DEVELOP ANY KIND OF SWING CONSISTENCY.

JM

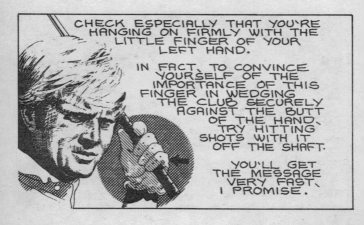

CHECK ESPECIALLY THAT YOU'RE HANGING ON FIRMLY WITH THE LITTLE FINGER OF YOUR LEFT HAND.

IN FACT, TO CONVINCE YOURSELF OF THE IMPORTANCE OF THIS FINGER IN WEDGING THE CLUB SECURELY AGAINST THE BUTT OF THE HAND, TRY HITTING SHOTS WITH IT OFF THE SHAFT.

YOU'LL GET THE MESSAGE VERY FAST, I PROMISE.

Let Hands Work Reflexively

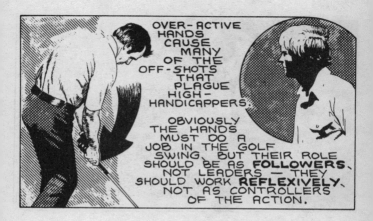

OVER-ACTIVE HANDS CAUSE MANY OF THE OFF-SHOTS THAT PLAGUE HIGH-HANDICAPPERS.

OBVIOUSLY THE HANDS MUST DO A JOB IN THE GOLF SWING, BUT THEIR ROLE SHOULD BE AS **FOLLOWERS**, NOT LEADERS — THEY SHOULD WORK **REFLEXIVELY**, NOT AS CONTROLLERS OF THE ACTION.

TO "FEEL" THE PROPER ROLE OF THE HANDS, CONSCIOUSLY TRY TO MAKE THEM PASSIVE IN RELATION TO YOUR ARM, BODY AND LEG ACTION WHILE HITTING EASILY WITH A SHORT-IRON.

THINKING OF THE HANDS SIMPLY AS A HINGE OR CONNECTING LINK BETWEEN YOUR ARMS AND THE CLUB WILL HELP YOU DEVELOP THE PROPER **REFLEXIVE** HAND ACTION.

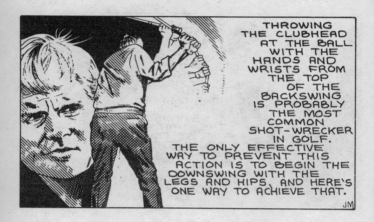

THROWING THE CLUBHEAD AT THE BALL WITH THE HANDS AND WRISTS FROM THE TOP OF THE BACKSWING IS PROBABLY THE MOST COMMON SHOT-WRECKER IN GOLF. THE ONLY EFFECTIVE WAY TO PREVENT THIS ACTION IS TO BEGIN THE DOWNSWING WITH THE LEGS AND HIPS, AND HERE'S ONE WAY TO ACHIEVE THAT.

JM

WORK ON THE FEELING OF TURNING THE SHOULDERS FULLY, THEN KEEPING THEM **FULLY COILED** AS LONG AS YOU POSSIBLY CAN WHILE YOUR KNEES MOVE TARGETWARDS AND YOUR HIPS UNWIND.

IT WILL TAKE EFFORT AND PRACTICE IF YOU ARE A HABITUAL "THROWER," BUT THE BENEFITS WILL BE IMMENSE.

Don't Let the Years Limit Your Swing

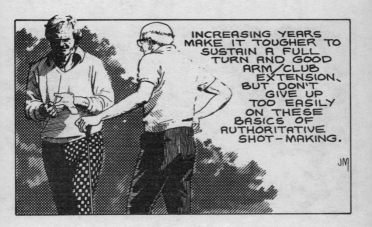

INCREASING YEARS MAKE IT TOUGHER TO SUSTAIN A FULL TURN AND GOOD ARM/CLUB EXTENSION. BUT DON'T GIVE UP TOO EASILY ON THESE BASICS OF AUTHORITATIVE SHOT-MAKING.

JM

RATHER THAN RELYING ON SIMPLY YOUR HANDS AND ARMS TO SWING THE CLUB, IF YOU'RE A SENIOR TRY LETTING YOUR **HIPS TURN** MORE FULLY ALONG WITH YOUR SHOULDERS GOING BACK.

REMEMBER, SO LONG AS YOU DON'T SWAY YOUR BODY OR LOOSEN YOUR GRIP YOU WON'T LOSE CONTROL OVER THE CLUB — AND YOU MAY WELL REGAIN SOME VERY USEFUL DISTANCE.

Tuck Right Elbow for Later Hit

IF YOU TEND TO HIT "EARLY" WITH YOUR HANDS AND WRISTS, CHECK YOUR RIGHT ARM AND SHOULDER DOWNSWING ACTION.

IF THE RIGHT ELBOW FLIES FORWARD, OR THE SHOULDER RIDES TOO HIGH — OR BOTH — YOU'RE ALMOST BOUND TO "HIT FROM THE TOP."

PRACTICE KEEPING YOUR RIGHT ELBOW TUCKED IN RIGHT UP UNTIL IMPACT. THE CLOSER YOU CAN KEEP IT TO YOUR BODY COMING DOWN, THE MORE YOU'LL BE ABLE TO SWING YOUR RIGHT SHOULDER "UNDER" YOUR HEAD — AND THE LATER THAT WILL ALLOW YOU TO RELEASE YOUR WRISTS.

Don't "Poke" with Your Irons

HIT YOUR WOODS BETTER THAN YOUR IRONS MUCH OF THE TIME?

COULD BE YOU ARE SUFFERING FROM THAT COMMON WEEKENDER'S DISEASE, "ACCURACY-ANXIETY."

IN OTHER WORDS, YOU'RE POKING AT THE BALL WITH THE IRONS BECAUSE YOU'RE OVERLY DIRECTION-CONSCIOUS.

CURE IS TO THINK OF SWINGING THE CLUB THROUGH THE BALL TO THE TARGET, INSTEAD OF TRYING TO "PLACE" THE BALL ON A PARTICULAR SPOT BY HITTING AT IT. AIM AND ALIGN YOURSELF PROPERLY, THEN LET IT ALL GO AS FREELY AS YOU DO WITH THE WOODS.

YOU MAY STILL MISS A FEW TARGETS, BUT NOT AS MANY AS BY TRYING TO STEER THE BALL TO THEM.

Beware Swinging Too Flat

A VERY COMMON FAULT AMONG HIGH HANDICAPPERS IS A FLAT OR HORIZONTAL SHOULDER TURN AWAY FROM THE BALL. THIS CAUSES THE LEFT ELBOW TO FLY FORWARD – TOWARDS THE BALL – AND THE CLUB TO BE PICKED UP WITH THE HANDS AND ARMS AND "LAID OFF" AT THE TOP.

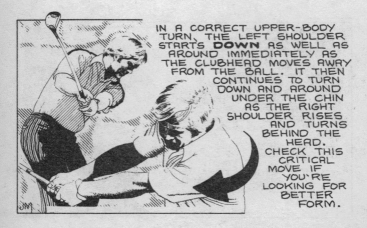

IN A CORRECT UPPER-BODY TURN, THE LEFT SHOULDER STARTS **DOWN** AS WELL AS AROUND IMMEDIATELY AS THE CLUBHEAD MOVES AWAY FROM THE BALL. IT THEN CONTINUES TO TURN DOWN AND AROUND UNDER THE CHIN AS THE RIGHT SHOULDER RISES AND TURNS BEHIND THE HEAD. CHECK THIS CRITICAL MOVE IF YOU'RE LOOKING FOR BETTER FORM.

Don't Be an Outward Looper

QUITE A NUMBER OF GOOD GOLFERS LOOP THE CLUB **INWARD** AT SOME POINT IN THE SWING.

ONLY POOR GOLFERS LOOP IT _OUTWARD_, ALWAYS WITH PAINFUL RESULTS.

COMMON CAUSE OF OUTWARD LOOPING OR "THROWING" IS SWAYING RATHER THAN TURNING THE HIPS GOING BACK. THIS CAUSES SPINNING AROUND THE RIGHT HIP STARTING DOWN, WHICH FORCES THE CLUB FORWARD BEYOND ITS CORRECT ARC.

CURE LIES IN _TURNING_ THE HIPS GOING BACK, THEN _SLIDE-TURNING_ THEM GOING DOWN AND THROUGH.

"LAY OFF" THE CLUB AT THE TOP OF THE BACKSWING AND YOU ENCOURAGE AN <u>OUTSIDE-IN</u> CLUBHEAD PATH AT IMPACT.

CONVERSELY, "CROSS THE LINE" AT THE TOP AND YOU RISK AN <u>INSIDE-OUT</u> ATTACK ON THE BALL.

IDEAL CLUB POSITION AT THE TOP IS POINTING DIRECTLY AT THE TARGET.

THUS ALIGNED, NO SWING COMPENSATION OR CLUB MANIPULATION IS NECESSARY TO DELIVER THE CLUBHEAD TO THE BALL TRAVELING <u>ALONG</u>, RATHER THAN ACROSS, THE TARGET LINE AT IMPACT.

JM

Firm Wrists to Prevent Over-Swing

SWINGING TOO FAR BACK CAN CAUSE CLUBHEAD DECELERATION BEFORE IMPACT UNLESS A GOLFER IS VERY SUPPLE OR WELL COORDINATED.

JM

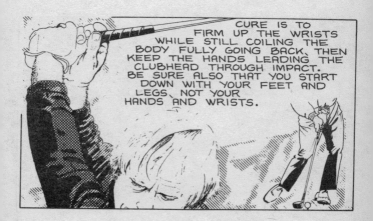

CURE IS TO FIRM UP THE WRISTS WHILE STILL COILING THE BODY FULLY GOING BACK, THEN KEEP THE HANDS LEADING THE CLUBHEAD THROUGH IMPACT. BE SURE ALSO THAT YOU START DOWN WITH YOUR FEET AND LEGS, NOT YOUR HANDS AND WRISTS.

8

Hitting Farther

TRY THIS APPROACH WHEN YOU NEED AN EXTRA BIG DRIVE.

FIRST, **RELAX** — LET YOUR MUSCLES GO AS LOOSE AND EASY AS POSSIBLE AS YOU WALK TO THE TEE. NEXT, AVOID ANY BUILD UP OF TENSION BY BEGINNING THE SWING AS SOON AS YOU FEEL COMFORTABLY SET UP TO THE BALL.

FINALLY, TRY TO SWING THE CLUB AWAY FROM THE BALL AS **LEISURELY** AND **DELIBERATELY** AS POSSIBLE.

I THINK YOU'LL FIND THIS "EASY" APPROACH ADDS USEFUL EXTRA YARDAGE — — BUT KEEP THE BIG ONES FOR WHEN ACCURACY ISN'T A KEY FACTOR.

EASY does it

Tee the Ball Higher

TIME AND AGAIN I SEE PRO-AM PARTNERS GIVING UP YARDS ON DRIVES SIMPLY BY TEEING THE BALL TOO **LOW**.

THE PICTURE TELLS WHY: THE LOWER YOU TEE THE BALL, THE MORE **DOWNWARD** RATHER THAN DIRECTLY FORWARD YOU'LL APPLY THE FORCE OF THE CLUBHEAD.

FOR MAXIMUM DISTANCE WITH THE DRIVER, TEE THE BALL SO THAT ITS EQUATOR IS AT LEAST LEVEL WITH THE TOP OF THE CLUBFACE.

THEN TRY TO POSITION THE BALL IN YOUR STANCE WHERE THE CLUB WILL MEET IT WHILE TRAVELING EITHER AT THE EXACT BOTTOM OF THE ARC OR VERY SLIGHTLY UPWARD.

Adjust Your Stance

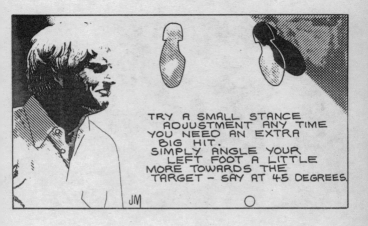

TRY A SMALL STANCE ADJUSTMENT ANY TIME YOU NEED AN EXTRA BIG HIT.
SIMPLY ANGLE YOUR LEFT FOOT A LITTLE MORE TOWARDS THE TARGET — SAY AT 45 DEGREES.

JM

POSITIONING THE LEAD FOOT THUS HAS THE EFFECT OF ACCELERATING THE LOWER BODY UNCOILING DURING THE DOWN-SWING, WHICH INCREASES LEVERAGE AND THEREBY CLUBHEAD SPEED.

BUT BE SURE TO KEEP YOUR UPPER BODY WELL BEHIND THE BALL AS YOUR LOWER HALF GOES TO WORK.

Hit Through, Not to, the Ball

HITTING **AT**, NOT **THROUGH**, THE GOLF BALL IS ONE OF THE MOST COSTLY FAULTS YOU CAN COMMIT IN TERMS OF BOTH LOST DISTANCE AND OFF-LINE TRAJECTORY.

IT SEEMS PARTICULARLY PREVALENT AMONG AMATEURS WITH THE WOODS AND LONG IRONS.

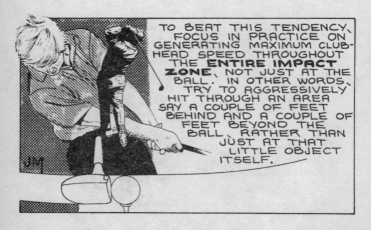

TO BEAT THIS TENDENCY, FOCUS IN PRACTICE ON GENERATING MAXIMUM CLUB-HEAD SPEED THROUGHOUT THE **ENTIRE IMPACT ZONE**, NOT JUST AT THE BALL. IN OTHER WORDS, TRY TO AGGRESSIVELY HIT THROUGH AN AREA SAY A COUPLE OF FEET BEHIND AND A COUPLE OF FEET BEYOND THE BALL, RATHER THAN JUST AT THAT LITTLE OBJECT ITSELF.

Seek a More Solid Strike

HOW FAR YOU CAN HIT THE BALL IS DETERMINED BY HOW **FAST** YOU CAN SWING THE CLUBHEAD **SQUARELY** THROUGH IT.

THROUGH PRACTICE, A FEW GOLFERS COULD DEVELOP MORE CLUBHEAD SPEED AND STILL HIT SQUARELY. BUT MOST LONG HANDICAPPERS WOULD GET MORE DISTANCE BY SACRIFICING A LITTLE CLUBHEAD SPEED FOR A MORE SOLID CLUBFACE DELIVERY.

2-2

Increase Your Swing Arc

WANT MORE DISTANCE?

THE BIGGER YOUR SWING ARC, THE BETTER YOUR CHANCE OF DRIVING THE BALL LONG.

THAT'S WHY I CULTIVATE THE FEELING OF EXTENDING MY LEFT ARM AS FULLY AS POSSIBLE AS I COMPLETE THE BACKSWING.

MANY GOLFERS CRAMP THEM-SELVES BY TRYING TO OVER-CONTROL THE SWING.

AS LONG AS YOU DON'T SWAY OR RAISE YOUR HEAD AND UPPER BODY, OR LOOSEN YOUR GRIP, **"REACHING FOR THE SKY"** SHOULD ADD POWER TO YOUR SHOTS WITHOUT LOSS OF ACCURACY.

Work on a Full Upper-Body Coil

WANT TO HIT FARTHER?

HERE'S MY FORMULA: **DISTANCE** COMES FROM CLUBHEAD SPEED SQUARELY APPLIED, CLUBHEAD SPEED COMES FROM LEVERAGE, AND LEVERAGE COMES FROM TORSION OR TORQUE.

JM

THEREFORE, THE FARTHER AND TIGHTER YOU CAN WIND THE UPPER PART OF YOUR BODY AGAINST THE RESISTANCE OF YOUR LOWER HALF, THE BETTER THE CHAIN REACTION AND THE GREATER THE CLUBHEAD SPEED YOU'LL CREATE.

SO WORK ON COILING YOURSELF FULLY GOING BACK.

Go Back Before You Start Down

SOMETIMES BOTH GREAT ACCURACY **AND** MAXIMUM DISTANCE ARE ESSENTIAL ON A DRIVE. IN THOSE CIRCUMSTANCES MY PRIMARY CONCERN IS TO START THE CLUB BACK FROM THE BALL AS SLOWLY AND SMOOTHLY AS I POSSIBLY CAN.

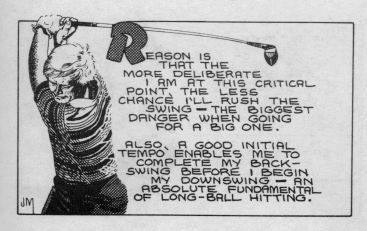

REASON IS THAT THE MORE DELIBERATE I AM AT THIS CRITICAL POINT, THE LESS CHANCE I'LL RUSH THE SWING — THE BIGGEST DANGER WHEN GOING FOR A BIG ONE.

ALSO, A GOOD INITIAL TEMPO ENABLES ME TO COMPLETE MY BACK-SWING BEFORE I BEGIN MY DOWNSWING — AN ABSOLUTE FUNDAMENTAL OF LONG-BALL HITTING.

JM

LOSING DISTANCE AS TIME MARCHES ON?

IF YOU'VE ALWAYS TENDED TO SLICE OR FADE THE BALL THERE'S A SURE WAY TO DELAY THAT PROCESS, BUT IT WILL PROBABLY REQUIRE BOTH WORK AND PATIENCE.

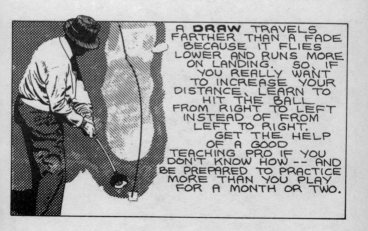

A **DRAW** TRAVELS FARTHER THAN A FADE BECAUSE IT FLIES LOWER AND RUNS MORE ON LANDING. SO, IF YOU REALLY WANT TO INCREASE YOUR DISTANCE, LEARN TO HIT THE BALL FROM RIGHT TO LEFT INSTEAD OF FROM LEFT TO RIGHT.
GET THE HELP OF A GOOD TEACHING PRO IF YOU DON'T KNOW HOW -- AND BE PREPARED TO PRACTICE MORE THAN YOU PLAY FOR A MONTH OR TWO.

9

Slicing and Hooking, Pulling and Pushing

Match Clubface Aim and Clubhead Path . . .

HOW TO STOP slicing OR hooking

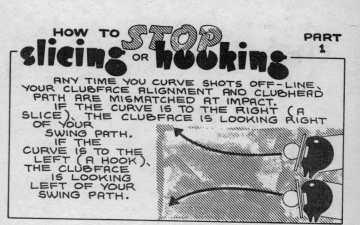

ANY TIME YOU CURVE SHOTS OFF-LINE, YOUR CLUBFACE ALIGNMENT AND CLUBHEAD PATH ARE MISMATCHED AT IMPACT.

IF THE CURVE IS TO THE RIGHT (A SLICE), THE CLUBFACE IS LOOKING RIGHT OF YOUR SWING PATH.

IF THE CURVE IS TO THE LEFT (A HOOK), THE CLUBFACE IS LOOKING LEFT OF YOUR SWING PATH.

USUALLY THIS MISMATCHING IS THE RESULT OF A FAULTY GRIP. IF YOU SLICE, MOVE BOTH HANDS GRADUALLY MORE TO THE **RIGHT** UNTIL THE BALL FLIES STRAIGHT IN THE SAME DIRECTION AS IT STARTS, WHICH WILL BE TO THE LEFT OF TARGET. REVERSE THAT PROCESS — MOVE YOUR HANDS GRADUALLY <u>LEFT</u> — IF YOU PREDOMINANTLY HOOK SHOTS.

HOW TO *STOP*
slicing or hookins

PART 2

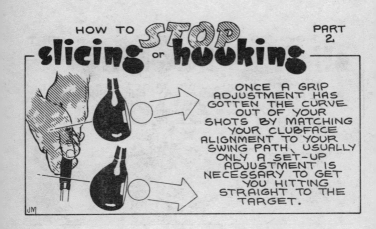

ONCE A GRIP ADJUSTMENT HAS GOTTEN THE CURVE OUT OF YOUR SHOTS BY MATCHING YOUR CLUBFACE ALIGNMENT TO YOUR SWING PATH, USUALLY ONLY A SET-UP ADJUSTMENT IS NECESSARY TO GET YOU HITTING STRAIGHT TO THE TARGET.

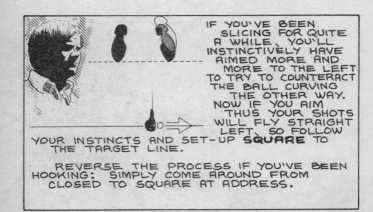

IF YOU'VE BEEN SLICING FOR QUITE A WHILE, YOU'LL INSTINCTIVELY HAVE AIMED MORE AND MORE TO THE LEFT TO TRY TO COUNTERACT THE BALL CURVING THE OTHER WAY. NOW IF YOU AIM THUS YOUR SHOTS WILL FLY STRAIGHT LEFT, SO FOLLOW YOUR INSTINCTS AND SET-UP **SQUARE** TO THE TARGET LINE.

REVERSE THE PROCESS IF YOU'VE BEEN HOOKING: SIMPLY COME AROUND FROM CLOSED TO SQUARE AT ADDRESS.

Always Double-Check Address Alignment

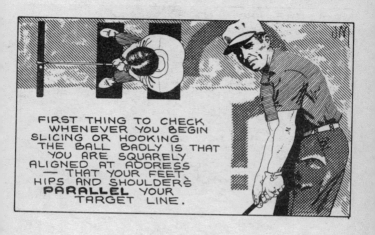

FIRST THING TO CHECK WHENEVER YOU BEGIN SLICING OR HOOKING THE BALL BADLY IS THAT YOU ARE SQUARELY ALIGNED AT ADDRESS — THAT YOUR FEET, HIPS AND SHOULDERS **PARALLEL** YOUR TARGET LINE.

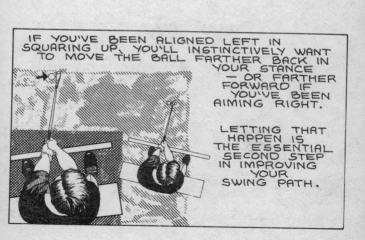

IF YOU'VE BEEN ALIGNED LEFT IN SQUARING UP, YOU'LL INSTINCTIVELY WANT TO MOVE THE BALL FARTHER BACK IN YOUR STANCE — OR FARTHER FORWARD IF YOU'VE BEEN AIMING RIGHT.

LETTING THAT HAPPEN IS THE ESSENTIAL SECOND STEP IN IMPROVING YOUR SWING PATH.

GOLFERS WHO SLICE MANY SHOTS AND ALSO SHANK OCCASION-ALLY WITH THE IRONS CAN BE SURE THE PROBLEM LIES IN THEIR UPPER-BODY ACTION STARTING THE DOWNSWING. "CASTING" WITH THE HANDS, AND HITTING WITH THE SHOULDERS FROM THE TOP, THROWS THE CLUB OUTWARD AND ACROSS THE TARGET LINE FROM OUT-TO-IN. WHEN THE OUTWARD MOVEMENT IS PARTICULARLY SEVERE, CONTACT IS ON THE HOSEL RATHER THAN THE CLUB'S BLADE.

THE CURE TO BOTH PROBLEMS LIES IN KEEPING THE UPPER BODY QUIETER OR MORE PASSIVE, AND USING THE LEGS AND HIPS TO **PULL** THE CLUB DOWN, RATHER THAN THROWING IT OUTWARD AT THE BALL.

WATCH THE TOUR PROS TO GET THE FEEL OF THIS VITAL GOLFING MOVE.

Try This "Band-Aid" if You Must

EVER BEEN SUDDENLY STRUCK WITH A CRIPPLING **SLICE** — BAD ENOUGH TO MAKE YOU WONDER IF YOU'LL HAVE ENOUGH BALLS TO COMPLETE THE ROUND??

HERE'S A "BAND-AID" TO AT LEAST GET YOU AS FAR AS THE PRO SHOP TO MAKE A DATE FOR A LESSON.

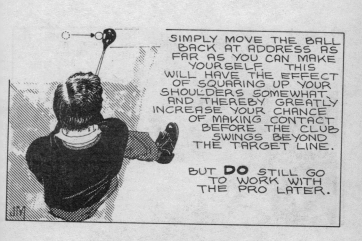

SIMPLY MOVE THE BALL BACK AT ADDRESS AS FAR AS YOU CAN MAKE YOURSELF. THIS WILL HAVE THE EFFECT OF SQUARING UP YOUR SHOULDERS SOMEWHAT, AND THEREBY GREATLY INCREASE YOUR CHANCE OF MAKING CONTACT BEFORE THE CLUB SWINGS BEYOND THE TARGET LINE.

BUT **DO** STILL GO TO WORK WITH THE PRO LATER.

JM

Consider Making Fade Work for You

JACK, I FADE OR SLICE JUST ABOUT EVERY SHOT. WHAT'S THE ANSWER?

YOU'VE GOT TWO CHOICES. EITHER LEARN TO STRIKE THE BALL WITHOUT CUTTING ACROSS IT FROM OUT TO IN. OR SIMPLY MAKE YOUR FADE WORK FOR YOU BY <u>ALLOWING</u> FOR IT.

IF YOU DON'T WANT TO RE-LEARN THE GAME, SIMPLY MAKE THE MOST OF WHAT YOU HAVE BY <u>AIMING</u> DOWN THE LEFT SIDE AND LETTING THE BALL SLICE BACK. YOU WON'T WIN A U.S. OPEN THAT WAY, BUT YOUR <u>SCORES</u> WILL IMPROVE.

TROUBLED WITH A HOOK? TRY SETTING THE CLUB MORE IN THE PALM OF YOUR LEFT HAND. THIS WILL FIRM UP YOUR WRIST ACTION THROUGH IMPACT, THEREBY DELAYING THE CLOSING OF THE CLUBFACE THROUGH THE BALL.

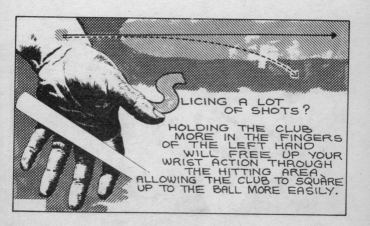

SLICING A LOT OF SHOTS?

HOLDING THE CLUB MORE IN THE FINGERS OF THE LEFT HAND WILL FREE UP YOUR WRIST ACTION THROUGH THE HITTING AREA, ALLOWING THE CLUB TO SQUARE UP TO THE BALL MORE EASILY.

PLAYING THE BALL TOO FAR BACK IN THE STANCE CAUSES HOOKING BY CREATING AN ACUTE INSIDE-OUT SWING PATH AND FORCING THE HANDS TO ROLL THE CLUBFACE CLOSED AS THEY STRIVE TO 'FIND' THE BALL.

SOLUTION IS TO MOVE THE BALL FORWARD IN THE STANCE LITTLE BY LITTLE DURING PRACTICE UNTIL THE RIGHT TO LEFT BENDS DISAPPEAR.

BALL POSITION MOST FAVORED FOR FULL SHOTS BY TOUR PLAYERS, INCLUDING ME, IS OPPOSITE OR JUST INSIDE THE LEFT HEEL.

Start to Swing Straight Back

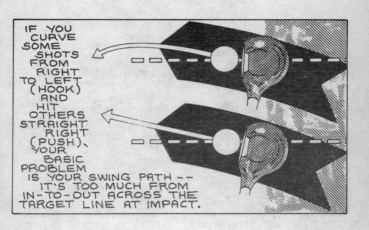

IF YOU CURVE SOME SHOTS FROM RIGHT TO LEFT (HOOK) AND HIT OTHERS STRAIGHT RIGHT (PUSH), YOUR BASIC PROBLEM IS YOUR SWING PATH -- IT'S TOO MUCH FROM IN-TO-OUT ACROSS THE TARGET LINE AT IMPACT.

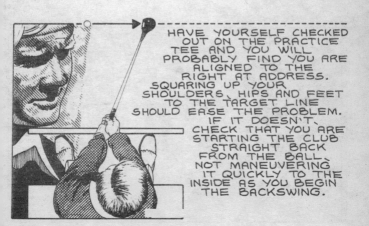

HAVE YOURSELF CHECKED OUT ON THE PRACTICE TEE AND YOU WILL PROBABLY FIND YOU ARE ALIGNED TO THE RIGHT AT ADDRESS. SQUARING UP YOUR SHOULDERS, HIPS AND FEET TO THE TARGET LINE SHOULD EASE THE PROBLEM. IF IT DOESN'T, CHECK THAT YOU ARE STARTING THE CLUB STRAIGHT BACK FROM THE BALL, NOT MANEUVERING IT QUICKLY TO THE INSIDE AS YOU BEGIN THE BACKSWING.

Check Your Left Wrist Action

GOT A SUDDEN CASE OF THE **HOOKS**??

IF YOU FEEL YOU ARE BASICALLY SWINGING WELL BUT THE BALL KEEPS CURVING TO THE LEFT, CHECK YOUR LEFT WRIST ACTION THROUGH IMPACT.

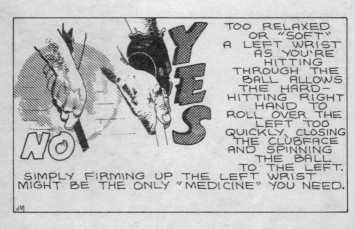

YES

NO

TOO RELAXED OR "SOFT" A LEFT WRIST AS YOU'RE HITTING THROUGH THE BALL ALLOWS THE HARD-HITTING RIGHT HAND TO ROLL OVER THE LEFT TOO QUICKLY, CLOSING THE CLUBFACE AND SPINNING THE BALL TO THE LEFT. SIMPLY FIRMING UP THE LEFT WRIST MIGHT BE THE ONLY "MEDICINE" YOU NEED.

JM

Improve Your Lower-Body Motion

THERE ARE A NUMBER OF CAUSES OF HOOKING, BUT ONE OF THE MOST PREVALENT IS INSUFFICIENT OR IMPROPER LOWER-BODY ACTION ON THE DOWNSWING.

TO PUT IT ANOTHER WAY, MANY GOLFERS HOOK SHOTS SIMPLY BY "GETTING IN THEIR OWN WAY."

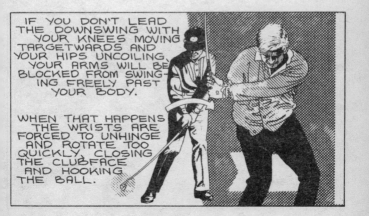

IF YOU DON'T LEAD THE DOWNSWING WITH YOUR KNEES MOVING TARGETWARDS AND YOUR HIPS UNCOILING, YOUR ARMS WILL BE BLOCKED FROM SWINGING FREELY PAST YOUR BODY.

WHEN THAT HAPPENS THE WRISTS ARE FORCED TO UNHINGE AND ROTATE TOO QUICKLY, CLOSING THE CLUBFACE AND HOOKING THE BALL.

Beware Trying to "Kill" the Ball

A DUCK-HOOK IS A SHOT WHERE THE BALL DIVES QUICKLY LEFT AND EARTHWARD AFTER TRAVELING ONLY SOME 50 TO 100 YARDS.

MAJOR CAUSE OF THIS HIGHLY DESTRUCTIVE SHOT IS WHIRLING THE BODY AROUND FROM THE TOP OF THE BACKSWING, OFTEN AS THE RESULT OF TRYING TO HIT HARDER.

CURE IS BETTER DOWNSWING-INITIATING LEG ACTION, COMBINED WITH MORE PASSIVE SHOULDERS AND HANDS UNTIL CENTRIFUGAL FORCE NATURALLY CAUSES THE CLUBHEAD TO BE RELEASED.

Focus on the Swing Path

IF YOU ARE MISDIRECTING THE BALL BADLY — PARTICULARLY PULLING OR PUSHING IT STRAIGHT LEFT OR RIGHT — HERE'S A TIP THAT MIGHT HELP YOU.

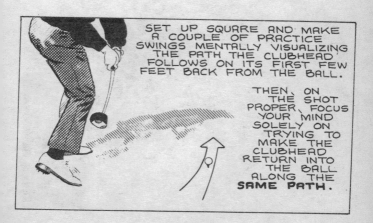

SET UP SQUARE AND MAKE A COUPLE OF PRACTICE SWINGS MENTALLY VISUALIZING THE PATH THE CLUBHEAD FOLLOWS ON ITS FIRST FEW FEET BACK FROM THE BALL.

THEN, ON THE SHOT PROPER, FOCUS YOUR MIND SOLELY ON TRYING TO MAKE THE CLUBHEAD RETURN INTO THE BALL ALONG THE **SAME PATH.**

Move Your Weight Faster

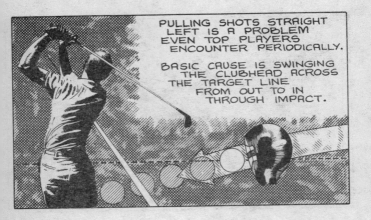

PULLING SHOTS STRAIGHT LEFT IS A PROBLEM EVEN TOP PLAYERS ENCOUNTER PERIODICALLY.

BASIC CAUSE IS SWINGING THE CLUBHEAD ACROSS THE TARGET LINE FROM OUT TO IN THROUGH IMPACT.

FREQUENT CAUSE OF THAT FAULT IS TOO LATE A WEIGHT TRANSFER TO THE LEFT SIDE DURING THE DOWNSWING.

CURE IS TO CONCENTRATE ON SHIFTING YOUR WEIGHT SMARTLY BUT SMOOTHLY TO YOUR LEFT, WHILE SWINGING YOUR RIGHT SHOULDER <u>DOWN AND UNDER</u> A <u>STEADY</u> HEAD.

Make Sure You Coil Fully

INSUFFICIENT SHOULDER TURN IS THE CHIEF CAUSE OF A PULL OR PULL-HOOK.

WHEN THEY'RE INSUFFICIENTLY TURNED GOING BACK, YOUR SHOULDERS UNWIND _TOO FAR TOO_ _FAST_ IN THE DOWNSWING, CAUSING AN OUT-TO-IN SWING PATH AT IMPACT.

IN ADDITION TO MAKING A FULL BACKSWING TURN, IT'S IMPORTANT FOR THE PULLER OR PULL-HOOKER TO WORK AT MAKING THE SHOULDERS LAG MOMENTARILY BEHIND THE LEG ACTION STARTING DOWN.

SEEK THE FEELING THAT THE LOWER BODY IS PULLING THE UPPER BODY ALONG AFTER IT, NOT THE OTHER WAY AROUND.

Check Ball Position if You're Pushing

IF YOU PUSH OR PUSH-SLICE A LOT OF SHOTS TO THE RIGHT, CHECK YOUR BALL POSITION AT ADDRESS. COULD BE SITUATING THE BALL TOO FAR BACK IN YOUR STANCE IS CAUSING YOU TO HIT IT WHILE THE CLUB IS STILL TRAVELING TO THE RIGHT OF — RATHER THAN STRAIGHT ALONG — THE TARGET LINE.

CONVERSELY, IF YOU PULL OR PULL-HOOK A LOT OF SHOTS, COULD BE THE BALL IS TOO FAR FORWARD, CAUSING THE CLUB TO STRIKE IT AFTER IT'S STARTED BACK TO THE LEFT OF THE TARGET LINE.

FINDING THE BALL POSITION THAT COINCIDES WITH YOUR CLUBHEAD PATH MOMENTARILY PARALLELING YOUR TARGET LINE CAN SOLVE A TON OF DIRECTIONAL PROBLEMS.

Don't "Get in Your Own Way"

"BLOCKING" SHOTS TO THE RIGHT, WITH OCCASIONAL DUCK HOOKS THROWN IN?

COULD BE YOU'RE NOT GETTING OUT OF YOUR OWN WAY AS YOU SWING THROUGH THE BALL.

IF YOUR HIPS DON'T UNCOIL TARGETWARDS AS YOUR KNEES LEAD THE DOWNSWING, YOU'LL MAKE INSUFFICIENT ROOM FOR YOUR ARMS TO SWING FREELY PAST YOUR BODY.

RESULT GENERALLY IS EITHER A SHOT PUSHED RIGHT IF YOUR WRISTS DON'T ROLL OVER THROUGH IMPACT, OR A FAST HOOK TO THE LEFT IF THEY DO.

10

Other Mis-hits

Check Your Weight Distribution

Don't Rise Up Coming Down

COMING OFF THE BALL?

THE SYMPTOMS ARE TOPPING, SLICING AND PULLING — ALTHOUGH ANY KIND OF MIS-HIT CAN RESULT.

JM

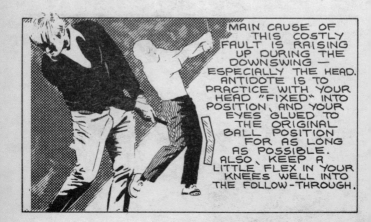

MAIN CAUSE OF THIS COSTLY FAULT IS RAISING UP DURING THE DOWNSWING — ESPECIALLY THE HEAD. ANTIDOTE IS TO PRACTICE WITH YOUR HEAD "FIXED" INTO POSITION, AND YOUR EYES GLUED TO THE ORIGINAL BALL POSITION FOR AS LONG AS POSSIBLE. ALSO, KEEP A LITTLE FLEX IN YOUR KNEES WELL INTO THE FOLLOW-THROUGH.

Understand What Causes a Shank

ANY GOLFER WHO SHANKS THE BALL MORE THAN VERY OCCASIONALLY NEEDS PROFESSIONAL HELP BECAUSE HE DEFINITELY POSSESSES SOME MAJOR SWING FLAWS.

BASIC CAUSE OF SHANKING IS MOVING THE PLANE OF THE SWING **OUTWARD** COMING DOWN.

STANDING TOO CLOSE TO THE BALL CAN PRODUCE THIS SOUL-DESTROYING SHOT, IN THAT IT FORCES THE ARMS OUTWARD IN ORDER TO SWING PAST THE BODY.

SO CAN STANDING TOO FAR FROM THE BALL, BY CAUSING THE GOLFER TO "THROW" THE CLUBHEAD FROM THE TOP, OR TO TOPPLE FORWARD DURING THE DOWNSWING, OR BOTH.

To Stop Shanking, Look to Your Head . . .

A **SHANK** IS CAUSED BY THE HOSEL RATHER THAN THE FACE OF THE CLUB CONTACTING THE BALL.

IT'S BY FAR THE WORST SHOT IN GOLF — IN FACT, IF IT BECOMES HABITUAL, IT MAKES THE GAME VIRTUALLY IMPOSSIBLE.

A LOT OF SWING FACTORS CAN CAUSE OR CONTRIBUTE TO A SHANK. HOWEVER, THE <u>UNDERLYING</u> FACTOR IN MOST CASES I'VE SEEN IS HEAD MOTION.

LINE UP AT A REASONABLE DISTANCE FROM THE BALL — NEITHER REACHING NOR CROWDING — AND <u>KEEP YOUR HEAD STEADY</u> THROUGHOUT THE SWING, AND YOU WILL VERY RARELY SHANK A SHOT.

My LIFELONG TEACHER, JACK GROUT, HAD AN EFFECTIVE WAY OF CURING SHANKING.

FIRST, HE'D ASK THE SUFFERER TO ADDRESS THE BALL OPPOSITE THE TOE OF THE CLUB AND THEN TRY TO HIT IT THERE.

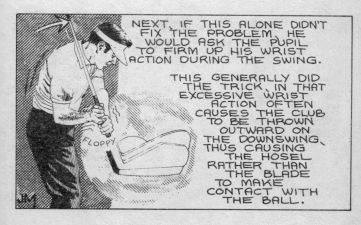

NEXT, IF THIS ALONE DIDN'T FIX THE PROBLEM, HE WOULD ASK THE PUPIL TO FIRM UP HIS WRIST ACTION DURING THE SWING.

THIS GENERALLY DID THE TRICK, IN THAT EXCESSIVE WRIST ACTION OFTEN CAUSES THE CLUB TO BE THROWN OUTWARD ON THE DOWNSWING, THUS CAUSING THE HOSEL RATHER THAN THE BLADE TO MAKE CONTACT WITH THE BALL.

FLOPPY

JM

137

Sweep Club Back Low to Stop "Skying"

"SKIED" OR "BALLOONED" SHOTS ARE THE RESULT OF HITTING DOWN INTO THE BALL TOO STEEPLY.

THIS IS CAUSED IN NUMEROUS WAYS, ONE OF THE MOST COMMON BEING A TOO-EARLY COCKING OF THE WRISTS IN THE BACKSWING.

THIS CREATES A VERY ABRUPT ARC BOTH AWAY FROM AND BACK TO THE BALL THAT CAN RESULT IN ALL SORTS OF IMPACT FAULTS, AS WELL AS "SKYING."

CURE IS TO START THE CLUB BACK LOW TO THE GROUND IN A <u>ONE-PIECE</u> HANDS/ARM/SHOULDERS SWEEPING MOTION. TRY TO ALLOW YOUR WRISTS TO COCK ONLY IN RESPONSE TO THE SWINGING MOMENTUM OF THE CLUBHEAD.

Move Ball and Head Back to Quit "Thinking"

HITTING A LOT OF SHOTS "THIN" WITH AN OCCASIONAL FULL-BLOODED TOP? TRY MOVING BOTH THE **BALL** AND YOUR **HEAD** A LITTLE FARTHER BACK (AWAY FROM THE TARGET) AT ADDRESS.

AND **KEEP** YOUR HEAD BACK THERE AS YOU SWING DOWN AND THROUGH.

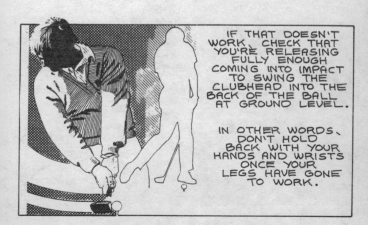

IF THAT DOESN'T WORK, CHECK THAT YOU'RE RELEASING FULLY ENOUGH COMING INTO IMPACT TO SWING THE CLUBHEAD INTO THE BACK OF THE BALL AT GROUND LEVEL.

IN OTHER WORDS, DON'T HOLD BACK WITH YOUR HANDS AND WRISTS ONCE YOUR LEGS HAVE GONE TO WORK.

Keep Fixed Axis to Stop Hitting "Fat"

LOOK FOR AWAY-FROM-THE-TARGET HEAD AND BODY SWAY GOING BACK WHENEVER YOU CATCH THE GROUND BEHIND THE BALL.

ANY UPPER BODY MOVEMENT AWAY FROM THE TARGET DURING THE BACKSWING OBVIOUSLY MOVES THE ENTIRE <u>ARC</u> OF THE SWING BACKWARDS ALSO.

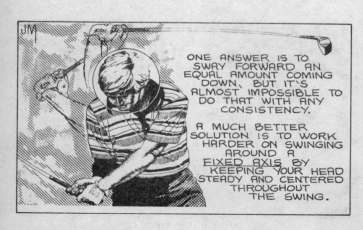

ONE ANSWER IS TO SWAY FORWARD AN EQUAL AMOUNT COMING DOWN, BUT IT'S ALMOST IMPOSSIBLE TO DO THAT WITH ANY CONSISTENCY.

A MUCH BETTER SOLUTION IS TO WORK HARDER ON SWINGING AROUND A <u>FIXED AXIS</u> BY KEEPING YOUR HEAD STEADY AND CENTERED THROUGHOUT THE SWING.

Eliminate Reverse Weight Shift

TOPPED SHOTS — AND A LOT OF OTHER FAULTS — ARE OFTEN CAUSED BY THE REVERSE WEIGHT SHIFT SHOWN HERE ... THE "FIRE AND FALL BACK," AS IT'S OFTEN CALLED.

LESSONS FROM A PROFESSIONAL ARE GENERALLY THE BEST ANSWER TO THIS KIND OF ACTION.

JM

HOWEVER, IF YOU WANT TO TRY SOME SELF-HELP, THEN WORK ON GETTING YOUR WEIGHT ALMOST ENTIRELY OVER ONTO YOUR **LEFT** SIDE BEFORE THE CLUB MEETS THE BALL.

(LETTING YOUR WEIGHT MOVE FULLY TO THE RIGHT SIDE GOING BACK WILL HELP YOU MAKE THAT ESSENTIAL DOWNSWING SHIFT)

Lead Clubhead with Hands at Impact

HITTING
"**FAT**"??
TOPPING SHOTS??

BOTH THESE PROBLEMS CAN COME FROM ALLOWING THE CLUBHEAD TO GET AHEAD OF THE HANDS PRIOR TO IMPACT, AS IN THE ILLUSTRATION. OFTEN THE BASIC FAULT LIES AT ADDRESS.

SET-UP TO THE BALL WITH THE CLUBHEAD AHEAD OF THE HANDS AND INSTINCTIVELY YOU'LL DELIVER IT THAT WAY AT IMPACT.

TO CURE THE FAULT, ADDRESS THE BALL AS I DO WITH THE LEFT ARM AND CLUBSHAFT IN A STRAIGHT LINE, WHICH AUTOMATICALLY SETS THE HANDS WHERE THEY SHOULD BE AT IMPACT — A LITTLE AHEAD OF THE BALL.

Be Sure to Release in Time

VARIOUS SWING FAULTS CAN CAUSE **TOPPING** — HITTING THE BALL ABOVE ITS EQUATOR — BUT ONE OF THE MOST COMMON AMONG GOOD GOLFERS IS TRYING TO **KILL** SHOTS!!

IT'S NATURAL WHEN REALLY GOING FOR A BIG ONE TO ACCELERATE THE LEG AND HIP ACTION ON THE DOWNSWING, BUT THIS CAN EASILY OVERDELAY THE RELEASE OF THE CLUBHEAD, CAUSING WHAT YOU SEE HERE.

SO BE SURE TO RELEASE SOON ENOUGH WITH YOUR HANDS AND WRISTS WHEN YOU'RE SEEKING EXTRA DISTANCE.

11

Difficult Lies and Different Flights

Consider All the Options

SOMETIMES A DROP CLEAR AND AN UNPLAYABLE-LIE PENALTY IS THE ONLY WAY OUT OF A TROUBLE SITUATION.

BUT DON'T MAKE THAT DECISION BEFORE YOU'VE FULLY CONSIDERED ALL THE OPTIONS.

I'VE SAVED SHOTS MANY TIMES IN MY CAREER BY:

— PLAYING LEFT-HANDED.

— BOUNCING THE BALL BACK INTO PLAY OFF A WALL OR OTHER OBSTACLE.

— BUNTING THE BALL CLEAR WITH A PUTTER.

Adjust Thus for Ball Below Feet

HERE'S THE ROUTINE TO FOLLOW WHEN THE BALL IS BELOW THE LEVEL OF YOUR FEET.

1) BEND MORE AT THE KNEES AND WAIST, AND GRIP THE CLUB AS CLOSE TO ITS END AS POSSIBLE, TO ENABLE YOU TO GET WELL "DOWN" TO THE SHOT.

2) SET MOST OF YOUR WEIGHT ON YOUR HEELS TO HELP YOU STAY BALANCED.

3) SWING AS SMOOTHLY AND COMPACTLY AS YOU CAN, USING CHIEFLY YOUR HANDS AND ARMS — AND KEEP YOUR **HEAD VERY STILL.**

4) ALLOW FOR THE BALL TO FADE — THE MORE THE STEEPER THE SLOPE.

JM

And Like This for Ball Above Feet

HERE'S A CHECK-LIST OF THE CHIEF ADJUSTMENTS TO MAKE WHEN THE BALL IS ABOVE THE LEVEL OF YOUR FEET.

1) STAND MORE ERECT THAN USUAL AND CHOKE DOWN ON THE CLUB TO IMPROVE YOUR BALANCE.

2) SET YOUR WEIGHT MORE TOWARD YOUR TOES TO FURTHER IMPROVE YOUR BALANCE.

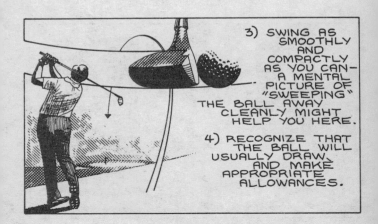

3) SWING AS SMOOTHLY AND COMPACTLY AS YOU CAN— A MENTAL PICTURE OF "SWEEPING" THE BALL AWAY CLEANLY MIGHT HELP YOU HERE.

4) RECOGNIZE THAT THE BALL WILL USUALLY DRAW, AND MAKE APPROPRIATE ALLOWANCES.

Strive for Balance on Downhill Lie

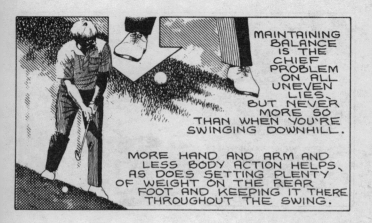

MAINTAINING BALANCE IS THE CHIEF PROBLEM ON ALL UNEVEN LIES, BUT NEVER MORE SO THAN WHEN YOU'RE SWINGING DOWNHILL.

MORE HAND AND ARM AND LESS BODY ACTION HELPS, AS DOES SETTING PLENTY OF WEIGHT ON THE REAR FOOT AND KEEPING IT THERE THROUGHOUT THE SWING.

BUT THE REAL KEY TO THIS SHOT IS STAYING DOWN AND CENTERED RIGHT THROUGH IMPACT, SO THAT YOU CAN REALLY "CHASE" THE CLUBHEAD DOWN THE SLOPE AND OUT AFTER THE BALL BEFORE YOUR BODY BEGINS TO LIFT OR FALL FORWARD.

JM

1219

BIG DANGER FROM A STEEP UPHILL LIE IS SWAYING THE BODY ON THE BACKSWING, WHICH CREATES A "FIRE AND FALL BACK" ROUTINE AND USUALLY EITHER A TOP OR "FAT" HIT.

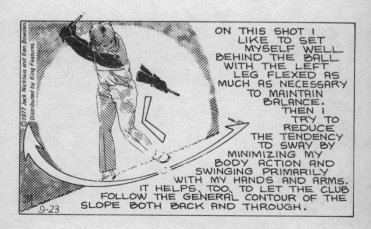

©1977 Jack Nicklaus and Ken Bowden. Distributed by King Features.

ON THIS SHOT I LIKE TO SET MYSELF WELL BEHIND THE BALL WITH THE LEFT LEG FLEXED AS MUCH AS NECESSARY TO MAINTAIN BALANCE. THEN I TRY TO REDUCE THE TENDENCY TO SWAY BY MINIMIZING MY BODY ACTION AND SWINGING PRIMARILY WITH MY HANDS AND ARMS. IT HELPS, TOO, TO LET THE CLUB FOLLOW THE GENERAL CONTOUR OF THE SLOPE BOTH BACK AND THROUGH.

9-23

Play Cut Shot from Hardpan

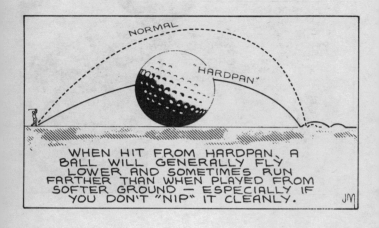

WHEN HIT FROM HARDPAN, A BALL WILL GENERALLY FLY LOWER AND SOMETIMES RUN FARTHER THAN WHEN PLAYED FROM SOFTER GROUND — ESPECIALLY IF YOU DON'T "NIP" IT CLEANLY.

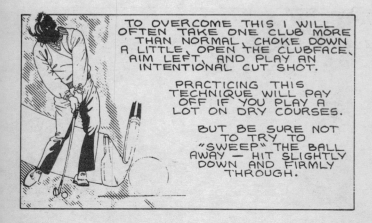

TO OVERCOME THIS I WILL OFTEN TAKE ONE CLUB MORE THAN NORMAL, CHOKE DOWN A LITTLE, OPEN THE CLUBFACE, AIM LEFT, AND PLAY AN INTENTIONAL CUT SHOT.

PRACTICING THIS TECHNIQUE WILL PAY OFF IF YOU PLAY A LOT ON DRY COURSES.

BUT BE SURE NOT TO TRY TO "SWEEP" THE BALL AWAY — HIT SLIGHTLY DOWN AND FIRMLY THROUGH.

Try Bunker Technique from Loose Material

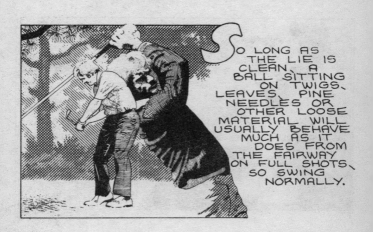

So long as the lie is clean, a ball sitting on twigs, leaves, pine needles or other loose material will usually behave much as it does from the fairway on full shots, so swing normally.

Around the green, loose materials react pretty much like soft sand when the ball is hit with anything less than full force, so consider playing a bunker-type shot.

In both cases, you will minimize the risk of incurring a penalty for moving the ball if you avoid grounding the club at address.

Punch Ball from Divot Mark

FIRST THINGS **NOT** TO DO WHEN CONFRONTED WITH A BALL IN A DIVOT MARK ARE FUME OR PANIC.

NEITHER ONE IS CONDUCIVE TO A GOOD RECOVERY STROKE.

SAFEST APPROACH TO THIS "RUB OF THE GREEN" IS A **PUNCH** SHOT. GO DOWN AT LEAST ONE AND POSSIBLY TWO CLUBS (7 TO A 6 OR 5, FOR EXAMPLE); PLAY THE BALL BACK MORE TOWARDS THE RIGHT FOOT; USE A THREE-QUARTER SWING PICKING THE CLUB UP SHARPLY STARTING BACK; AND SWING SHARPLY DOWN INTO THE BALL WITHOUT LETTING YOUR WRISTS ROLL OVER UNTIL WELL AFTER IMPACT.

ALLOW FOR A LOW TRAJECTORY AND LOTS OF RUN.

"Feel" Swing Length When Restricted

KEY TO PLAYING ANY SHOT WITH A RESTRICTED BACKSWING IS TO MAKE PLENTY OF "MEASURING" PRACTICE SWINGS TO GET THE FEEL OF THE ABBREVIATED STROKE.

ONCE YOU'VE GOT A SENSE OF HOW FAR YOU CAN LET THE CLUB SWING BACK, FORGET THE OBSTACLE THAT'S RESTRICTING YOU AND CONCENTRATE ON WATCHING THE BALL CLOSELY AND STRIKING IT CLEANLY.

IT'S TRUE THAT THE PROS CAN SOMETIMES BEST CONTROL RECOVERY SHOTS FROM LIGHT OR MEDIUM ROUGH WITH THE LONGER IRONS, ESPECIALLY THOSE PLAYERS WHO NATURALLY SWING ON A FAIRLY UPRIGHT PLANE.

FOR AVERAGE GOLFERS, HOWEVER, THE BEST BETS FROM ALMOST ANY TYPE OF ROUGH ARE THE WELL-LOFTED WOODEN CLUBS, SIMPLY BECAUSE THEIR ROUNDED SOLES CUT THROUGH LONG GRASS A LOT MORE EASILY THAN THE STRAIGHT LEADING EDGES OF LONG IRONS.

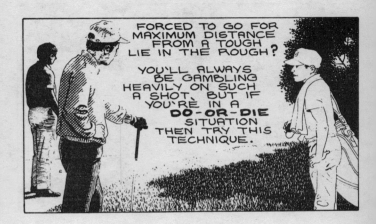

FORCED TO GO FOR MAXIMUM DISTANCE FROM A TOUGH LIE IN THE ROUGH?

YOU'LL ALWAYS BE GAMBLING HEAVILY ON SUCH A SHOT, BUT IF YOU'RE IN A **DO-OR-DIE** SITUATION THEN TRY THIS TECHNIQUE.

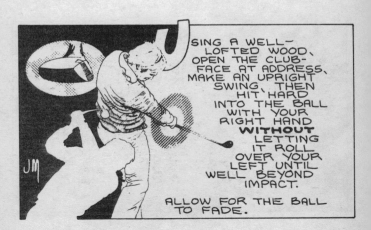

USING A WELL-LOFTED WOOD, OPEN THE CLUB-FACE AT ADDRESS, MAKE AN UPRIGHT SWING, THEN HIT HARD INTO THE BALL WITH YOUR RIGHT HAND **WITHOUT** LETTING IT ROLL OVER YOUR LEFT UNTIL WELL BEYOND IMPACT.

ALLOW FOR THE BALL TO FADE.

JM

HERE'S A SHOT TO CONSIDER WHEN YOU NEED MAXIMUM DISTANCE FROM ROUGH OR A POOR FAIRWAY LIE AND DIRECTION ISN'T CRITICAL — AS, FOR INSTANCE, ON THE SECOND SHOT ON A WIDE—OPEN PAR—FIVE.

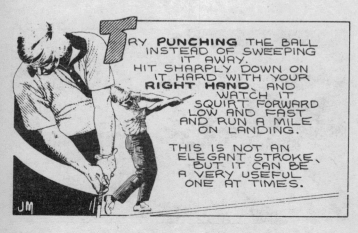

TRY **PUNCHING** THE BALL INSTEAD OF SWEEPING IT AWAY. HIT SHARPLY DOWN ON IT HARD WITH YOUR **RIGHT HAND**, AND WATCH IT SQUIRT FORWARD LOW AND FAST AND RUN A MILE ON LANDING.

THIS IS NOT AN ELEGANT STROKE, BUT IT CAN BE A VERY USEFUL ONE AT TIMES.

Don't Panic Over a Sandy Lie

DON'T PANIC ANY TIME YOU ENCOUNTER A SANDY LIE IN THE ROUGH, EVEN THOUGH THE LIE MAY LOOK FRIGHTENINGLY TIGHT.

TRY THE FOLLOWING TECHNIQUE, ESPECIALLY WHEN THE SAND IS FIRM.

BURROW YOUR CLEATS WELL INTO THE SAND AND FIRM UP YOUR STANCE TO ENSURE STABILITY. PLAY THE BALL BACK TOWARD THE CENTER OF YOUR FEET, GRIP FIRMLY WITH YOUR LEFT HAND, SWING THE CLUB UP A LITTLE MORE ABRUPTLY THAN NORMAL — AND **FOLLOW-THROUGH.**

FIRM

Take Less Club from a "Flier" Lie

BE AWARE OF WHAT WILL HAPPEN TO THE BALL ANY TIME YOU HIT IT FROM THICK VEGETATION — CLOVER PARTICULARLY AFFECTS A SHOT BECAUSE OF ITS SPIN-REDUCING "GREASINESS."

CONFRONTED WITH A "FLIER" LIE, TAKE ONE LESS CLUB TO COMPENSATE FOR LOWER FLIGHT AND ADDITIONAL RUN. THEN, IN SWINGING, TRY TO HIT **DOWN** MORE WITH YOUR HANDS TO ENSURE YOU GET THE CLUBFACE AS FULLY ONTO THE BACK OF THE BALL AS POSSIBLE.

MOST OF ALL, DON'T EXPECT MIRACLES — PLAY THE SAFE SHOT.

Play Lob Shot for Extra "Stop"

STOPPING THE BALL QUICKLY BY APPLYING HEAVY BACKSPIN FROM ROUGH IS ALWAYS DIFFICULT, AND SOMETIMES IMPOSSIBLE. GIVEN A LIE WHERE THE BALL SITS FAIRLY WELL ATOP A CUSHION OF GRASS, I DON'T TRY.

INSTEAD, I PLAY A LOB-TYPE SHOT, POSITIONING THE BALL FARTHER FORWARD IN MY STANCE, THEN RELEASING THE CLUBHEAD EARLY FOR A MORE SWEEPING CONTACT WITH THE LOWER BACK PART OF THE BALL. PROPERLY EXECUTED, THE RESULT IS A HIGH, "FLOATING" TYPE SHOT THAT SETTLES QUICKLY EVEN THOUGH IT CARRIES LITTLE BACKSPIN.

Consider Direction of Grass Growth

DIRECTION OF GRASS GROWTH CAN BE A BIG FACTOR IN SHOTS FROM ROUGH.

WHEN THE GRAIN IS LYING AGAINST YOU, TRY TO HIT "UNDER" THE BALL AS MUCH AS POSSIBLE — LIKE YOU WOULD FOR A HIGH SHOT.

USE ONE OR TWO CLUBS MORE THAN NORMAL TO COUNTERACT THE DISTANCE YOU'LL LOSE.

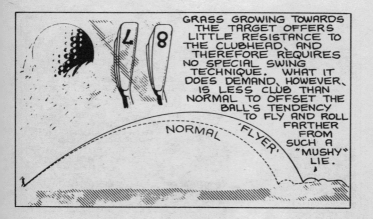

GRASS GROWING TOWARDS THE TARGET OFFERS LITTLE RESISTANCE TO THE CLUBHEAD, AND THEREFORE REQUIRES NO SPECIAL SWING TECHNIQUE. WHAT IT DOES DEMAND, HOWEVER, IS LESS CLUB THAN NORMAL TO OFFSET THE BALL'S TENDENCY TO FLY AND ROLL FARTHER FROM SUCH A "MUSHY" LIE.

NORMAL

"FLYER"

Tee the Ball Higher

YOU'LL FREQUENTLY ENCOUNTER THE NEED FOR EXTRA HEIGHT ON AN IRON SHOT ON A PAR-THREE HOLE — AS, FOR INSTANCE, IN THE SITUATION SHOWN HERE, WHERE THE BALL MUST BE STOPPED VERY QUICKLY.

TEEING THE BALL A LITTLE HIGHER THAN NORMAL CAN HELP YOU GET ADDITIONAL HEIGHT BY PROMOTING A MORE **SWEEPING** ACTION THROUGH IMPACT — ESPECIALLY WITH THE MEDIUM AND LONG IRONS. TRY IT ON THE PRACTICE TEE TO FAMILIARIZE YOURSELF WITH THE EFFECT.

ONE OF MY GREATEST ASSETS THROUGHOUT MY CAREER HAS BEEN THE ABILITY TO HIT THE BALL HIGH WITH ALL THE CLUBS. THIS IS PARTICULARLY HELPFUL ON LONG APPROACH SHOTS, WHERE BOTH DISTANCE AND STOPPING POWER ARE REQUIRED.

JM

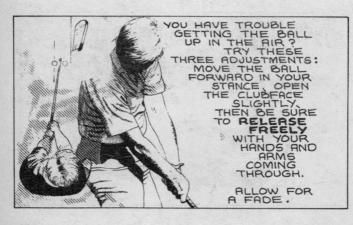

YOU HAVE TROUBLE GETTING THE BALL UP IN THE AIR? TRY THESE THREE ADJUSTMENTS: MOVE THE BALL FORWARD IN YOUR STANCE, OPEN THE CLUBFACE SLIGHTLY, THEN BE SURE TO **RELEASE FREELY** WITH YOUR HANDS AND ARMS COMING THROUGH.

ALLOW FOR A FADE.

Check Your Body Action

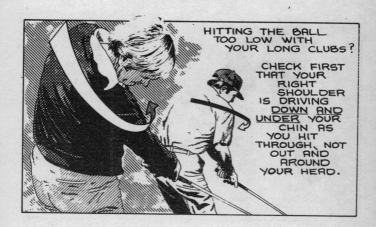

HITTING THE BALL TOO LOW WITH YOUR LONG CLUBS?

CHECK FIRST THAT YOUR RIGHT SHOULDER IS DRIVING <u>DOWN AND UNDER</u> YOUR CHIN AS YOU HIT THROUGH, NOT OUT AND AROUND YOUR HEAD.

IF THIS DOESN'T ADD HEIGHT AND CARRY, HAVE SOMEONE CHECK YOUR HEAD AND UPPER BODY MOTION THROUGH THE HITTING AREA.

ANY FORWARD MOVEMENT OF YOUR TOP HALF COMING DOWN AND THROUGH WILL PROMOTE A DELOFTING OF THE CLUBFACE — NOT TO MENTION A HOST OF OTHER FAULTS.

Hit the Ball Lower Like This

TO KEEP THE BALL LOW, I SIMPLY MOVE IT BACK IN RELATION TO MY FEET AT ADDRESS, THEN KEEP MY HANDS LEADING THE CLUBFACE A LITTLE LONGER THAN NORMAL THROUGH IMPACT.

TENDENCY IN PLAYING THIS SHOT IS TO HOOK OR DRAW THE BALL, ESPECIALLY WITH THE STRAIGHTER-FACED CLUBS. SO THE BEST POLICY IS TO ALLOW FOR A LITTLE RIGHT-TO-LEFT CURVE.

2-11

12

Combating
Bad Weather

MOST GOLFERS RECOGNIZE THAT REALLY BAD WEATHER REQUIRES MODIFICATIONS IN TECHNIQUE, AND TRY TO MAKE THEM TO THE BEST OF THEIR ABILITY.

WHAT MANY DON'T MAKE, HOWEVER, IS A PROPER MENTAL ADJUSTMENT TO THE REALITIES OF SCORING UNDER ROUGH CONDITIONS.

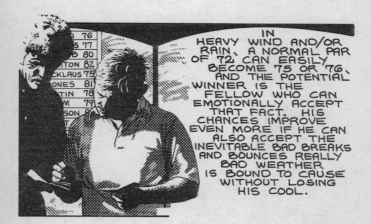

IN HEAVY WIND AND/OR RAIN, A NORMAL PAR OF 72 CAN EASILY BECOME 75 OR 76, AND THE POTENTIAL WINNER IS THE FELLOW WHO CAN EMOTIONALLY ACCEPT THAT FACT. HIS CHANCES IMPROVE EVEN MORE IF HE CAN ALSO ACCEPT THE INEVITABLE BAD BREAKS AND BOUNCES REALLY BAD WEATHER IS BOUND TO CAUSE WITHOUT LOSING HIS COOL.

Match Flight to Wind Conditions . . .

WHENEVER YOU NEED MAXIMUM DISTANCE HITTING INTO A HEADWIND, TRY TO MOVE THE BALL FROM RIGHT TO LEFT...

... IN OTHER WORDS, SET UP AND SWING FOR A DRAW RATHER THAN A STRAIGHT SHOT OR A FADE.

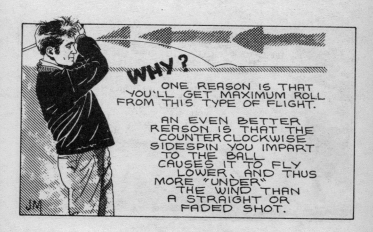

WHY?

ONE REASON IS THAT YOU'LL GET MAXIMUM ROLL FROM THIS TYPE OF FLIGHT.

AN EVEN BETTER REASON IS THAT THE COUNTERCLOCKWISE SIDESPIN YOU IMPART TO THE BALL CAUSES IT TO FLY LOWER, AND THUS MORE "UNDER" THE WIND THAN A STRAIGHT OR FADED SHOT.

IN A BIG WIND THERE'S A NATURAL TENDENCY TO WIDEN THE STANCE TO ESTABLISH FIRMER FOOTING AND BETTER BALANCE. PROBLEM IS THAT THIS REDUCES BODY TURN AND SHORTENS THE BACK-SWING, THUS REDUCING DISTANCE.

JM

THE EASIEST SOLUTION IS SIMPLY TO TAKE ENOUGH CLUB TO OFFSET THE EFFECT OF THE MORE COMPACT SWING. THIS HAS THE ADDITIONAL ADVANTAGE OF KEEPING THE BALL LOW AND THUS LESS AFFECTED BY THE WIND.

Consider Driver from Fairway

WITH A HARD WIND AGAINST ME, OR ACROSS ME, I'LL OFTEN CONSIDER HITTING A DRIVER FROM THE FAIRWAY INSTEAD OF A THREE-WOOD, TO REDUCE THE CHANCE OF THE BALL "BALLOONING" AND SO BEING HELD SHORT AND BLOWN OFF LINE.

A GOOD LIE IS ESSENTIAL, HOWEVER.

JM

THIS IS NEVER AN EASY SHOT, BUT YOU'LL FIND IT CONSIDERABLY LESS DIFFICULT IF YOU CHOKE WELL DOWN ON THE DRIVER GRIP, THEREBY INCREASING YOUR CONTROL AND AT THE SAME TIME ENSURING A LOW AND BORING FLIGHT.

ALSO, SWING **SMOOTHLY** — AND NEVER TRY TO FORCE THE SHOT.

Play Straight in Wet Conditions

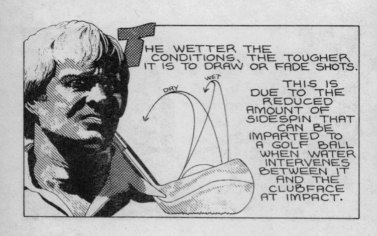

THE WETTER THE CONDITIONS, THE TOUGHER IT IS TO DRAW OR FADE SHOTS.

THIS IS DUE TO THE REDUCED AMOUNT OF SIDESPIN THAT CAN BE IMPARTED TO A GOLF BALL WHEN WATER INTERVENES BETWEEN IT AND THE CLUBFACE AT IMPACT.

PROS CALL SHOTS THAT ARE INTENDED TO CURVE INTO THE TARGET BUT DON'T DO SO "SLIDERS" AND THEY CAN BECOME REAL SCORE-WRECKERS IF YOU TRY TO GET TOO FANCY IN WET WEATHER.

BEST STRATEGY IS TO TRY TO HIT THE BALL AS STRAIGHT AS POSSIBLE WITH EVERY CLUB.

AY CAREFUL ATTENTION TO YOUR FOOTING WHEN PLAYING IN WET OR MUDDY CONDITIONS, BECAUSE THE SLIGHTEST SLIP COULD PUT A VERY LARGE NUMBER ON YOUR SCORECARD.

ALWAYS ENSURE, FOR EXAMPLE, THAT YOUR SPIKES ARE CLEAN BEFORE STEPPING UP TO A SHOT.

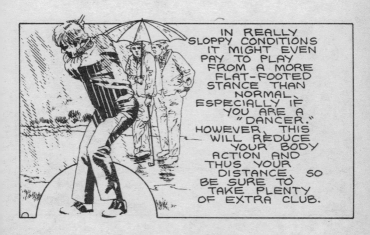

IN REALLY SLOPPY CONDITIONS IT MIGHT EVEN PAY TO PLAY FROM A MORE FLAT-FOOTED STANCE THAN NORMAL, ESPECIALLY IF YOU ARE A "DANCER." HOWEVER, THIS WILL REDUCE YOUR BODY ACTION AND THUS YOUR DISTANCE, SO BE SURE TO TAKE PLENTY OF EXTRA CLUB.

HE MORE CLEANLY YOU CAN "PICK" THE BALL FROM SODDEN OR MUDDY GROUND, THE BETTER YOU WILL PLAY — ESPECIALLY WITH THE LONG AND MEDIUM IRONS.

CHOKING DOWN ON THE CLUB SLIGHTLY WILL PROMOTE A CLEANER STRIKE.

IN REALLY SWAMPY CONDITIONS, IT'S POSSIBLE YOU MIGHT EVEN SINK A LITTLE AS YOU ADDRESS THE BALL, GIVING YOU THE EFFECT OF A SLIGHT SIDEHILL LIE.

CHOKING DOWN ALSO HELPS TO OFFSET THIS VARIATION.

Hit from Water Like a Buried Sand Lie

THE MORE DEEPLY SUBMERGED THE BALL, THE WORSE YOUR CHANCE OF HITTING IT OUT OF THE WATER.

HOWEVER, IF YOU WANT TO TAKE YOUR CHANCE AND DON'T MIND GETTING WET (AND PROBABLY DIRTY), HERE IS THE TECHNIQUE TO TRY.

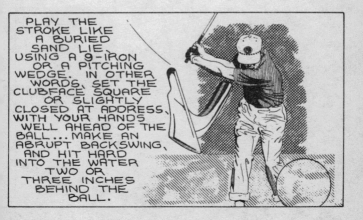

PLAY THE STROKE LIKE A BURIED SAND LIE USING A 9-IRON OR A PITCHING WEDGE. IN OTHER WORDS, SET THE CLUBFACE SQUARE OR SLIGHTLY CLOSED AT ADDRESS, WITH YOUR HANDS WELL AHEAD OF THE BALL...MAKE AN ABRUPT BACKSWING, AND HIT HARD INTO THE WATER TWO OR THREE INCHES BEHIND THE BALL.

Part THREE

The Short Game

13

Pitching
the Ball

Never Scoop!

TRYING TO GET THE BALL AIRBORNE BY SCOOPING UP AT IT WITH THE CLUBHEAD IS A COMMON FAULT OF NOVICE GOLFERS.

IT'S PARTICULARLY EVIDENT – AND DISASTROUS — ON SHORT PITCH AND CHIP SHOTS.

A GOLF BALL MUST BE STRUCK <u>DOWN</u> TO FLY **UP**. ONE SIMPLE WAY TO ENSURE THIS ON SHORT SHOTS IS TO SET THE HANDS AHEAD OF THE CLUBFACE AT <u>ADDRESS</u>, THEN <u>KEEP THEM THERE</u> THROUGHOUT THE STROKE. IF YOUR HANDS NEVER PASS YOUR CLUBFACE UNTIL AFTER IMPACT, IT'S ALMOST IMPOSSIBLE TO SCOOP AT THE BALL.

SO TRY <u>CONSCIOUSLY</u> LEADING WITH YOUR HANDS IF YOU'RE MIS-HITTING A LOT OF SHORT SHOTS.

Beware of Forcing Wedge Shots

WEEKEND PLAYERS MISS A LOT OF WEDGE SHOTS BY TRYING TO FORCE THE CLUB. THE WEDGE IS NOT A DISTANCE WEAPON — IT'S BUILT FOR FINESSING THE BALL.

IF YOU CAN'T GET HOME WITHOUT SWINGING IT FLAT-OUT, TAKE A BIGGER CLUB.

I RARELY TRY TO HIT A WEDGE MORE THAN 100 YARDS, AND NEITHER SHOULD YOU.

SWING THE CLUB **SMOOTHLY** AND WELL WITHIN YOURSELF, CONCENTRATING PARTICULARLY ON FIRM HAND ACTION THROUGH IMPACT.

FIRM

Swing the Club More Crisply

A LOT OF WEDGE SHOTS ARE MISSED AS A RESULT OF OVER-SWINGING GOING BACK, THEN SLOWING DOWN COMING THROUGH THE BALL. THIS IS PARTICULARLY EASY TO DO ON 'PART' SHOTS – ANYTHING REQUIRING LESS THAN YOUR FULL SWING ARC AND FORCE.

ONE WAY TO STRENGTHEN THIS AREA OF YOUR GAME IS TO DEVELOP A CRISPER STROKE BASED ON EXTRA WRIST ACTION. HOLD THE CLUB FIRMLY, KEEP THE BACKSWING AS SHORT AS POSSIBLE, THEN APPLY WHATEVER DEGREE OF EXTRA PUNCH IS REQUIRED WITH YOUR WRIST RELEASE THROUGH IMPACT. PRACTICE THIS 'FEEL' SHOT BEFORE YOU TAKE IT TO THE COURSE.

Set Weight More to the Left

IF YOU HAVE PROBLEMS WITH YOUR WEDGE PLAY, TRY SETTING MORE OF YOUR WEIGHT ON YOUR LEFT FOOT AT ADDRESS AND LEAVING IT THERE DURING THE BACKSWING.

THIS WILL HELP TO FIRM UP YOUR STRIKING ACTION BY CUTTING DOWN ON YOUR BODY MOTION.

EQUALLY IF NOT MORE IMPORTANT, IT WILL ENSURE THAT YOU SWING THE CLUB ON THE ABRUPT ARC NECESSARY TO HIT CRISPLY DOWN AND THROUGH THE BALL.

PLAYED CORRECTLY,
A SHORT PITCH FROM
AN UPHILL LIE — A
COMMON SHOT ON COURSES
WITH ELEVATED GREENS —
ISN'T AS TOUGH AS IT LOOKS.

KEY IS TO SET
YOURSELF AND SWING
SO THAT THE CLUB
FOLLOWS THE ANGLE
OF THE SLOPE
BACK AND THROUGH.

USE A SWEEPING
RATHER THAN A
PUNCHING ACTION
AND THE BALL WILL
CLIMB OUT SOFT
AND HIGH AND
STOP QUICKLY.

HIT A LITTLE
HARDER THAN
NORMAL TO
COMPENSATE FOR
THE HIGHER
TRAJECTORY.

Use Sand-Wedge from Tough Grass

HIGHER HANDICAP GOLFERS OFTEN HAVE A TENDENCY TO HIT "FAT" ON SHORT PITCH SHOTS, ESPECIALLY FROM TOUGH GRASSES LIKE BERMUDA WHERE IT'S EASY TO "STICK THE CLUB IN THE GROUND."

JM

ONE ANSWER TO THIS PROBLEM IS TO FAVOR YOUR **SAND-WEDGE** RATHER THAN YOUR PITCHING-WEDGE OR OTHER SHORT-IRONS. REASON? THE "BOUNCE" BUILT INTO THE SAND CLUB, VIA ITS PROTRUDING FLANGE, ENABLES IT TO SLIDE OVER RATHER THAN STICK IN THE GRASS IF YOU HIT DOWN A LITTLE TOO STEEPLY OR TOO FAR BEHIND THE BALL.

HITTING FORCE IS HARD TO JUDGE ON ANY LESS – THAN – FULL SHOT, BUT NEVER MORE SO THAN ON A HALF WEDGE PITCH OF BETWEEN 30 AND 50 YARDS.

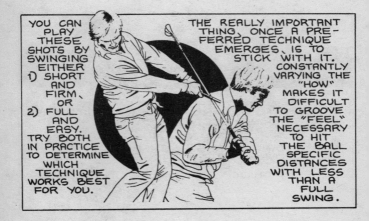

YOU CAN PLAY THESE SHOTS BY SWINGING EITHER 1) SHORT AND FIRM, OR 2) FULL AND EASY. TRY BOTH IN PRACTICE TO DETERMINE WHICH TECHNIQUE WORKS BEST FOR YOU.

THE REALLY IMPORTANT THING, ONCE A PREFERRED TECHNIQUE EMERGES, IS TO STICK WITH IT. CONSTANTLY VARYING THE "HOW" MAKES IT DIFFICULT TO GROOVE THE "FEEL" NECESSARY TO HIT THE BALL SPECIFIC DISTANCES WITH LESS THAN A FULL SWING.

14

Bunker Play

IN THIS OR SIMILARLY PROBLEMATICAL SAND SITUATIONS, FIX YOUR MIND ON THE FIRST RULE OF BUNKER PLAY BEFORE YOU DRAW THE CLUB BACK:

FIRST, GET THE BALL OUT!

DECIDE WHICH IS BETTER: BEING FORCED TO ATTEMPT MUCH THE SAME SHOT AGAIN. OR STANDING OVER A LONGISH PUTT AFTER HAVING TAKEN A LESS DIRECT BUT SAFER ROUTE. I CERTAINLY KNOW WHICH I'D PREFER!

Lose Your "Ball Fixation"

MANY HIGH-HANDICAPPERS SUFFER IN SAND TRAPS BECAUSE OF "BALL FIXATION"—THEY CAN'T MAKE THEMSELVES FOCUS BOTH MIND AND EYE ON HITTING INTO AND THROUGH THE SAND, RATHER THAN AT THE BALL ITSELF.

HERE'S A TIP THAT WILL HELP. ENVISION AN AREA OF SAND ABOUT THREE INCHES WIDE AND EIGHT INCHES LONG OF WHICH THE BALL IS PART. THEN, IN SETTING UP AND PLAYING THE SHOT, FOCUS MENTALLY ON REMOVING THE **ENTIRE OBLONG** OF SAND YOU ARE PICTURING. ACHIEVE THAT AND THERE'S NO WAY THE BALL CAN STAY IN THE BUNKER!

Set Up Slicing Action This Way

HERE'S A TIP THAT MIGHT TAKE MUCH OF THE TERROR OUT OF BUNKER SHOTS EXPERIENCED BY SO MANY BEGINNERS AND "RABBITS."

AT LEAST IT SHOULD ENSURE THAT YOU GET THE BALL OUT OF THE SAND IN ONE SHOT.

JM

AT ADDRESS, SET-UP OPEN (AIMED LEFT) OF WHERE YOU WANT THE BALL TO FINISH, THEN OPEN THE CLUBFACE - ALIGN IT TO THE RIGHT OF THE TARGET AN EQUIVALENT AMOUNT. YOU'VE NOW ESTABLISHED A SLICING ACTION OF THE CLUBHEAD THAT WILL EASILY REMOVE THE BALL IF YOU SIMPLY SWING NORMALLY AND HIT **SMOOTHLY** THROUGH THE SAND **BEHIND** IT.

Execute Sand Shots Purposefully

BUNKERED BESIDE THE GREEN?

USE YOUR SAND WEDGE, OPEN THE CLUBFACE, AIM A LITTLE LEFT OF TARGET, COCK YOUR WRISTS QUICKLY GOING BACK, THEN HIT FIRMLY THROUGH THE SAND UNDER THE BALL WITH YOUR RIGHT HAND.

DO THOSE FIVE THINGS GUARANTEE A SUCCESSFUL RECOVERY SHOT?

THE ANSWER IS 'YES' **ONLY** IF YOU HAVE SUFFICIENTLY OVERCOME ANY INHERENT FEAR OF SAND. YOU MAY HAVE TO EXECUTE THEM **PURPOSEFULLY.** FOR MOST GOLFERS, THAT WILL REQUIRE ACTUALLY PRACTICING THESE TECHNIQUES FOR A WHILE.

Think and Act in Slow Motion

THE BEST TIP I CAN OFFER ON RECOVERING FROM BUNKERS CONCERNS **ATTITUDE**, NOT METHOD.

INEXPERIENCE, ANXIETY AND PLAIN DISLIKE OF HAVING TO PLAY FROM SAND CAUSES MANY HANDICAP GOLFERS TO TRY TO GET THESE SHOTS OVER WITH AS FAST AS POSSIBLE.

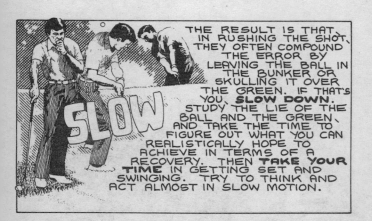

THE RESULT IS THAT, IN RUSHING THE SHOT, THEY OFTEN COMPOUND THE ERROR BY LEAVING THE BALL IN THE BUNKER OR SKULLING IT OVER THE GREEN. IF THAT'S YOU, **SLOW DOWN**. STUDY THE LIE OF THE BALL AND THE GREEN, AND TAKE THE TIME TO FIGURE OUT WHAT YOU CAN REALISTICALLY HOPE TO ACHIEVE IN TERMS OF A RECOVERY. THEN **TAKE YOUR TIME** IN GETTING SET AND SWINGING. TRY TO THINK AND ACT ALMOST IN SLOW MOTION.

Use Different Arcs for Different Lies

THE VERY ABRUPT ARC YOU SEE HERE IS USEFUL WHEN YOU HAVE TO "KNIFE" THE CLUB DOWN HARD UNDER A BALL BURIED IN SAND. COMBINE IT WITH A SQUARE CLUBFACE AND A VERY FIRM HIT.

HOWEVER, FOR A NORMAL EXPLOSION SHOT FROM A GOOD LIE, I PREFER THE MORE FLAT-BOTTOMED ARC THAT COMES FROM A NORMAL SWING, FIRST TO AVOID HITTING TOO CLOSE TO THE BALL, AND SECOND TO INSURE AGAINST TAKING TOO MUCH SAND.

KEEP THE CLUBFACE OPEN THROUGH IMPACT AND SWING SMOOTHLY.

Try for Distance Like This

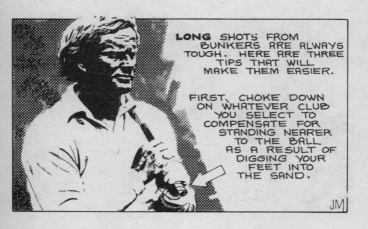

LONG SHOTS FROM BUNKERS ARE ALWAYS TOUGH. HERE ARE THREE TIPS THAT WILL MAKE THEM EASIER.

FIRST, CHOKE DOWN ON WHATEVER CLUB YOU SELECT TO COMPENSATE FOR STANDING NEARER TO THE BALL AS A RESULT OF DIGGING YOUR FEET INTO THE SAND.

JM

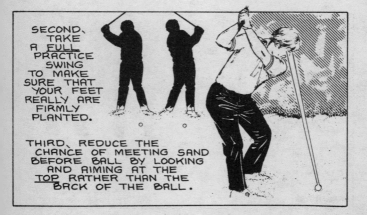

SECOND, TAKE A **FULL** PRACTICE SWING TO MAKE SURE THAT YOUR FEET REALLY ARE FIRMLY PLANTED.

THIRD, REDUCE THE CHANCE OF MEETING SAND BEFORE BALL BY LOOKING AND AIMING AT THE **TOP** RATHER THAN THE BACK OF THE BALL.

15

On the Green

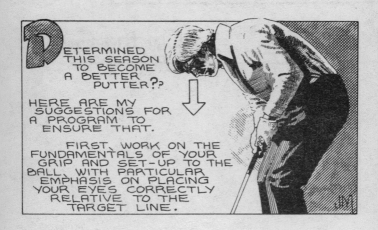

DETERMINED THIS SEASON TO BECOME A BETTER PUTTER??

HERE ARE MY SUGGESTIONS FOR A PROGRAM TO ENSURE THAT.

FIRST, WORK ON THE FUNDAMENTALS OF YOUR GRIP AND SET-UP TO THE BALL, WITH PARTICULAR EMPHASIS ON PLACING YOUR EYES CORRECTLY RELATIVE TO THE TARGET LINE.

NEXT, WORK ON THE STROKE ITSELF, CONCENTRATING ON SMOOTHNESS AND ON MEETING THE BALL CONSISTENTLY ON THE PUTTER'S SWEET SPOT. FINALLY, WORK ON JUDGING SPEED AND BREAK BY PRACTICING REGULARLY AND ON AS MANY DIFFERENT TYPES OF GREENS AS POSSIBLE.

Take Time for a Proper Survey

THE WAY MANY AMATEURS STEP UP AND HIT LONG PUTTS AFTER ONLY A CURSORY GLANCE AT THE LINE SOMETIMES MAKES YOU THINK THEY ENJOY THREE—PUTTING!

WET AND DRY SPOTS, CHANGING GRAIN DIRECTION AND SLOPE, VARYING GRASS THICKNESS — ALL WILL AFFECT THE BALL'S COURSE AND SPEED.

SO TAKE A FEW MOMENTS TO TAKE A GOOD LOOK AROUND — PREFERABLY WHILE YOUR PLAYING COMPANIONS ARE DOING THEIR OWN SURVEYING.

Check Your Eye Alignment

PERHAPS THE MOST IMPORTANT SINGLE FACTOR IN PUTTING FOR MOST GOLFERS IS THEIR EYE-LINE IN RELATION TO THE BALL.

IF YOUR EYES ARE OUT BEYOND THE BALL, YOU'LL TEND TO PULL PUTTS TO THE LEFT, AND IF THEY'RE INSIDE THE LINE YOU'LL TEND TO PUSH PUTTS TO THE RIGHT.

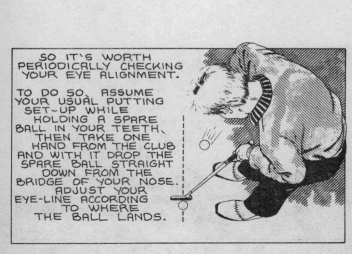

SO IT'S WORTH PERIODICALLY CHECKING YOUR EYE ALIGNMENT.

TO DO SO, ASSUME YOUR USUAL PUTTING SET-UP WHILE HOLDING A SPARE BALL IN YOUR TEETH, THEN TAKE ONE HAND FROM THE CLUB AND WITH IT DROP THE SPARE BALL STRAIGHT DOWN FROM THE BRIDGE OF YOUR NOSE. ADJUST YOUR EYE-LINE ACCORDING TO WHERE THE BALL LANDS.

VERY SMALL THINGS CAN MAKE VERY LARGE DIFFERENCES IN PUTTING, AND A CASE IN POINT IN MY GAME IS THE RIGHT **ELBOW.**

IF IT CREEPS AWAY FROM MY SIDE, I'LL TEND TO CLOSE THE FACE OF THE PUTTER AND ALSO SWING ACROSS THE TARGET LINE FROM OUTSIDE-TO-IN.

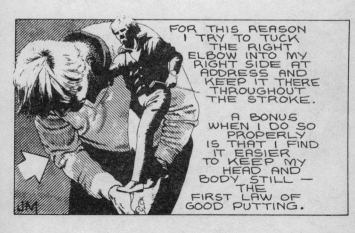

FOR THIS REASON I TRY TO TUCK THE RIGHT ELBOW INTO MY RIGHT SIDE AT ADDRESS AND KEEP IT THERE THROUGHOUT THE STROKE.

A BONUS WHEN I DO SO PROPERLY IS THAT I FIND IT EASIER TO KEEP MY HEAD AND BODY STILL — THE FIRST LAW OF GOOD PUTTING.

HERE ARE A COUPLE OF TIPS THAT MIGHT HELP YOU ON THE GREENS.

IF YOU ARE HAVING DIFFICULTY STROKING **THROUGH** (RATHER THAN TO) THE BALL, TRY POINTING YOUR LEFT ELBOW MORE TOWARDS THE HOLE.

THAT WAY YOU SHOULD FIND IT EASIER TO KEEP YOUR LEFT HAND MOVING FREELY TARGETWARDS THROUGH IMPACT.

IF YOUR PROBLEMS ARE MORE IN THE WAY OF NOT MAKING SOLID CONTACT WITH THE BALL, TRY SETTING YOUR LEFT ELBOW **CLOSER** IN TOWARDS YOUR LEFT SIDE.

THAT WAY YOU'LL FIND IT EASIER TO DELIVER A FIRM TAP WITH THE RIGHT HAND AS YOU STROKE THROUGH THE BALL.

ANYTIME THE BALL ISN'T ROLLING SMOOTHLY OFF THE PUTTER BLADE, CHECK THE ALIGNMENT OF YOUR PUTTER AT ADDRESS.

JM

LAYING THE SHAFT BACK AWAY FROM THE HOLE MAY BE CAUSING YOU TO CATCH THE BALL "THIN." CONVERSELY, TILTING THE SHAFT FORWARD — WHICH DELOFTS THE PUTTER FACE — MAY BE DRIVING THE BALL INTO THE GROUND AT IMPACT, CAUSING IT TO JUMP.

THAT'S WHY MOST GOOD PUTTERS TRY TO SET THE SHAFT PERPENDICULAR TO THE GROUND AS THEY ADDRESS THE BALL.

HAVE DIFFICULTY STARTING THE PUTTERHEAD AWAY FROM THE BALL SMOOTHLY? TENSION IS OFTEN THE PROBLEM, AND ONE WAY TO BREAK IT DOWN IS TO INITIATE THE BACKSWING OFF A SLIGHT FORWARD PRESS.

SIMPLY EASE YOUR WRISTS TOWARDS THE HOLE SLIGHTLY, THEN GO RIGHT INTO THE BACKSWING OFF THIS ACTION.

BUT DON'T OVER-DO THE FORWARD PRESSING MOTION OR YOU'LL OPEN THE FACE OF THE PUTTER.

JM

Accelerate *Through the Ball*

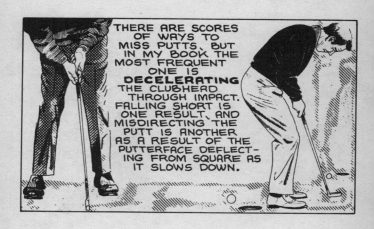

THERE ARE SCORES OF WAYS TO MISS PUTTS. BUT IN MY BOOK THE MOST FREQUENT ONE IS **DECELERATING** THE CLUBHEAD THROUGH IMPACT. FALLING SHORT IS ONE RESULT, AND MISDIRECTING THE PUTT IS ANOTHER AS A RESULT OF THE PUTTERFACE DEFLECTING FROM SQUARE AS IT SLOWS DOWN.

SO DON'T BE TENTATIVE.

MAKE A FIRM, SMOOTH, CONTROLLED BACKSWING, THEN **ACCELERATE** RIGHT **THROUGH** THE BALL. A GOOD PRACTICE EXERCISE IS TO MAKE SURE THE CLUBHEAD FOLLOWS THROUGH AT LEAST A FOOT ON PUTTS OF SIX FEET OR LESS.

Work on Stroke to Master Speed

GOT THE PUTTING BLUES?

MOST THREE-PUTTS ARE THE RESULT OF LEAVING THE BALL SHORT OR HITTING IT TOO FAR, NOT OF KNOCKING IT WAY WIDE OF THE HOLE.

SO FIRST WORK ON **SPEED**, RATHER THAN ON LINE.

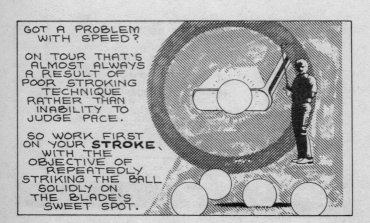

GOT A PROBLEM WITH SPEED?

ON TOUR THAT'S ALMOST ALWAYS A RESULT OF POOR STROKING TECHNIQUE RATHER THAN INABILITY TO JUDGE PACE.

SO WORK FIRST ON YOUR **STROKE**, WITH THE OBJECTIVE OF REPEATEDLY STRIKING THE BALL SOLIDLY ON THE BLADE'S SWEET SPOT.

Go with Your Instincts

GIVEN THE CHOICE, SHOULD YOU PUTT THE BALL OR CHIP IT FROM JUST OFF THE GREEN?

MY ADVICE WOULD BE TO GO WITH YOUR INSTINCTS, BECAUSE THEY PROBABLY REFLECT YOUR CONFIDENCE LEVEL IN THE TWO OPTIONS.

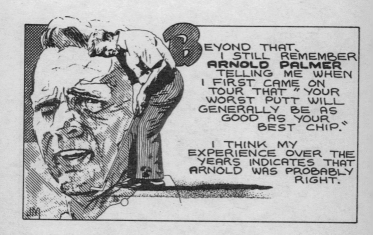

BEYOND THAT, I STILL REMEMBER **ARNOLD PALMER** TELLING ME WHEN I FIRST CAME ON TOUR THAT "YOUR WORST PUTT WILL GENERALLY BE AS GOOD AS YOUR BEST CHIP."

I THINK MY EXPERIENCE OVER THE YEARS INDICATES THAT ARNOLD WAS PROBABLY RIGHT.

Don't Be Too Bold on Downhill Putts

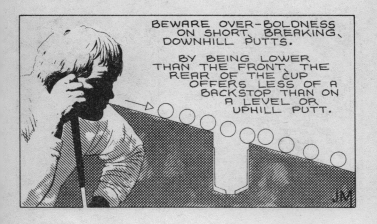

BEWARE OVER-BOLDNESS ON SHORT, BREAKING, DOWNHILL PUTTS.

BY BEING LOWER THAN THE FRONT, THE REAR OF THE CUP OFFERS LESS OF A BACKSTOP THAN ON A LEVEL OR UPHILL PUTT.

JM

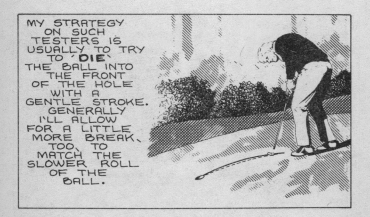

MY STRATEGY ON SUCH TESTERS IS USUALLY TO TRY TO 'DIE' THE BALL INTO THE FRONT OF THE HOLE WITH A GENTLE STROKE. GENERALLY I'LL ALLOW FOR A LITTLE MORE BREAK, TOO, TO MATCH THE SLOWER ROLL OF THE BALL.

Learn to "Feel" Speed on Long Putts

A VERY LONG PUTT IS ONE OF GOLF'S TOUGHEST SHOTS.

HOW WELL YOU PLAY IT DEPENDS CHIEFLY ON HOW WELL YOU CAN MENTALLY "FEEL" THE SPEED YOU NEED TO IMPART TO THE BALL.

I'VE FOUND THAT STANDING A LITTLE TALLER OR MORE UPRIGHT OVER THE BALL AT ADDRESS HELPS ME IN SENSING SPEED, PROBABLY BY GIVING ME A BETTER VIEW OF THE DISTANCE TO BE COVERED.

ALSO, STANDING TALLER PROMOTES A FREER AND MORE FLUID STROKE.

Putt to More Than Cup Itself

DON'T BE TOO "HOLE-CONSCIOUS" ON VERY LONG PUTTS.

YOU MIGHT OCCASIONALLY MAKE A 40- OR 50-FOOTER, BUT ACTUALLY TRYING TO DO SO ALL THE TIME IS UNREALISTIC — AND CAN DEFINITELY LEAD TO THREE-PUTTING.

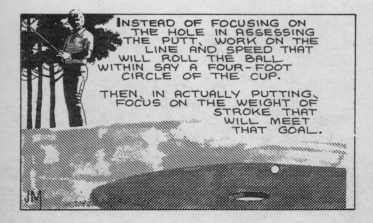

INSTEAD OF FOCUSING ON THE HOLE IN ASSESSING THE PUTT, WORK ON THE LINE AND SPEED THAT WILL ROLL THE BALL WITHIN SAY A FOUR-FOOT CIRCLE OF THE CUP.

THEN, IN ACTUALLY PUTTING, FOCUS ON THE WEIGHT OF STROKE THAT WILL MEET THAT GOAL.

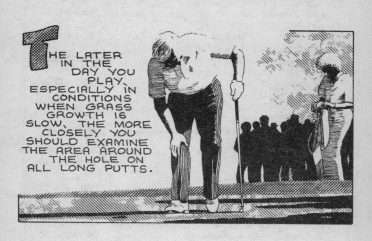

THE LATER IN THE DAY YOU PLAY, ESPECIALLY IN CONDITIONS WHEN GRASS GROWTH IS SLOW, THE MORE CLOSELY YOU SHOULD EXAMINE THE AREA AROUND THE HOLE ON ALL LONG PUTTS.

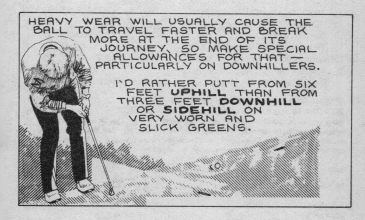

HEAVY WEAR WILL USUALLY CAUSE THE BALL TO TRAVEL FASTER AND BREAK MORE AT THE END OF ITS JOURNEY, SO MAKE SPECIAL ALLOWANCES FOR THAT — PARTICULARLY ON DOWNHILLERS.

I'D RATHER PUTT FROM SIX FEET **UPHILL** THAN FROM THREE FEET **DOWNHILL** OR **SIDEHILL** ON VERY WORN AND SLICK GREENS.

207